GOD AMENDS

By

Emman Goka

Shield Crest

© Copyright 2018 Emman Goka

ISBN 978-1-912505-17-3

MMXVIII

A CIP catalogue record for this book
is available from the British Library

Published by
ShieldCrest
Aylesbury, Buckinghamshire, HP18 0TF
England
www.shieldcrest.co.uk
+44 (0) 333 8000 890

Contents

Dedication

About this Book

Chapters

Dedication

Your consistency, principles and virtues are what make you different from the other many billions in the world.

I dedicate **God Amends** to you, Patrice, and to that sweet friend and sister, Stephanie, whose directions, laughter and smiles made New York warmer that week.

And also to all those men, and all those women, all those boys, and all those girls, who know that with both knees touching the floor or ground, and your heads bowed in petition, God amends.

About this book

Don't read *God Amends* only as a recreational novel. Read it with a deductive and questioning mind. It will enrich you more than a few moments of a (recreational) high. If you do that, you will gain understanding into mysteries that you must know. And with that understanding, you will be enveloped into a greater and blessed future and new Earth.

In *God Amends* you will be exposed to terms such as 'sexual health celebration' or 'sexual health sharing'. The two terms mean one and the same thing, and are used to refer to sexual relations between a woman and a man – a woman and a man who desire to understand the power, the authority, and the awesomeness of the mystery of sexual acts, and to obtain the multiple benefits when they actively play their roles mutually, as did the men and women in the novel who reaped enduring benefits.

Another term used is, 'the people of the nations in the various countries of the world', to refer to all other classes of people as distinct from the Melon Elembele family members.

Great reading, and share the knowledge you've gained with others, or buy *God Amends* as a gift for her or him.

CHAPTER 1

Knowing the gods

Philadelphia, PA, USA. October 16, 2017

Flight time was twenty-six hours. We were glad that Mr Melon Elembele had sent his personal aircraft to fly us to Mepoto Islands. And therefrom, to take a canoe to the Meba Village where the trial of seventeen missing men of the Melon Elembele family had taken place, and whose fate, though determined, had not taken place. The village elders and head chief were waiting for the next appearance of the quarter moon, to one by one administer the poison that first takes away speech of the condemned person, next causes paralysis of the upper limbs and then the lower limbs, and then the cutting off, if a woman, of her vulva and keeping it in the shrine of the Goka god. And if a man, removal of both testis and the male genitalia and hanging it erect pointing upwards in the shrine of the female god, Golu, whose right it is to give a condemned person's genitalia to an impotent villager to tie around his waist to have the potency to father a child.

Not two hours after our arrival, we were ushered in to meet the chief and elders. They gave us a drink, brownish in colour, that we could not and were advised not to refuse before we set out on the journey that we could not reject. We drank with smiles on our faces to show to our hosts that we appreciated their welcome hospitality.

We gave seventeen pairs of raffia mats to indicate the acceptance of their wise judgment in condemning members of our Melon Elembele family, who had trespassed into the village and

1

were seen in the company of seventeen women, who thought the men – the seventeen – were princes birthed through the marriage of the Goka and Golu (god and goddess), sent to marry them. But the first elder who saw them knew they were not men who should be in the company of the village's unmarried women. He therefore cast a spell on the men and they stood still where they were standing and chatting with the women and became clay statues. And before he could ask the women to leave, they fled in seventeen different directions towards the Lepo River to wash away the uncleanness that they brought on themselves by associating with what, in their village, they call 'rabiwy' – associating with men that should not have been associated with.

The elder went to inform the chief, who asked that the men be brought before him. The elder returned and merely spoke saying, "What are you doing here?" and they were changed into human form and followed him to the chief 's court. The chief asked for the seventeen women to be informed to attend a trial fixed for the next seventeen days – a day for each. Each man, at a twenty-foot distance from the line of seventeen women – was sentenced to death.

There was no mention of our names. We were identified with numbers and as numbers. The three of us were given the numbers 1, 2 and 4. We didn't know why they skipped 3. But we asked no question, not knowing the culture or the ways of these people. We didn't regard them as primitive or backward, or uneducated or unenlightened, because our granddad Melon Elembele had warned us that no member of his Melon Elembele family should because of not understanding another's culture or ways of doing things and thus feel superior or be condescending. "Hold your peace and learn and give room to understand," Granddad Melon Elembele had advised.

On the seventh night of our visit, we were suddenly summoned to the chief 's palace. He informed us that that night would be the night of nights, because we would witness, first-hand, the ebbing away of the lives of the seventeen men of our family whom he could not do anything to save because they were the prisoners or the condemned of the gods. He informed us that when the condemned are lined up to suffer their fate, one of us – but he quickly said, the number 4 – will lift their hoods from their faces one by one and shake each person's hand as a sign of farewell, thus committing them for a life in another world. We knelt before him, but our foreheads did not touch the floor as their custom demanded.

A thicket grove was where we were taken at 9pm that evening. At 10pm, they started bringing the condemned men, one at time. The last man was brought at 11:20pm. The poison was to be administered to disable the men before midnight and before the beginning of another day – so was explained to us at the thicket grove – and I was asked that, as the person numbered as 4, I must step forward to start the farewell ceremony of the handshake.

I moved from the other two to the first condemned man, and starting with the tallest among them I lifted his hood, and the moon shone strangely brighter for us to identify each other. He screamed, "Golu Goka!", and there was a shaking of the ground under our feet. I don't know whether it shook under the chief's feet also, or his assembled elders who were witnessing the ceremony.

I moved to the second condemned man, lifted his hood and shook his hand, and the moon brightened again for us to identify each other. He, not powerfully because I saw tears dripping from his face, said, "Golu Goka, is it the price to pay to admire and fall in love with a woman and chat with her?" The ground shook again. I turned to look at the other two who came with me on the trip and discerned that they too had felt the shaking of the ground as they had moved from where we originally stood. I then moved away from them. The chiefs and elders were at the original spot.

Next, I lifted the hood of the third condemned man and told him, "You will be the third to suffer death among a people you don't understand and who don't understand you." At the concluding of my statement, the moon shone like it did the first two times and he recognized me and said, "Golu Goka" to my

3

hearing. At that instant, an elder came forward to where I stood and said that the chief had heard the names of two gods been called out. I pretended I didn't hear him and he walked back. I took the fourth and fifth hoods off in like manner. The moon shone to expose my face for recognition. Each mentioned the names Golu Goka. The shaking of the ground was longer and more pronounced. I turned and saw the chief and elders conversing.

I took the sixth and seventh brothers through like acts and they also mentioned the names Golu Goka. The shaking of the earth was continuous. And I heard the sound of what sounded like wails of birds in mourning for the dead. The wailing was followed by rapturous clapping and singing of what sounded like young women celebrating the victory of the village men from war with a neighbouring village's men. But there were no women in sight to be seen and heard. I turned and saw the chief and elders take to flight as the song from the female voices was harping on the names of Golu Goka continuously.

The men, the seventeen, in unison took off their hoods and joined the unseen female singers in singing the names Golu Goka. We sang long and tired. And who should come into view in the thicket grove, but the seventeen women. Each went to a condemned man and embraced him. "Golu Goka are our female and male gods," the women said in unison.

And each couple danced the rest of the night away.

The next morning, the chief and elders came to our lodging place and apologized to the seventeen men and seventeen women. And then our flight took off for the return journey with other members for the Melon Elembele family. When at our destination and home, they all knelt, because my names, Golu Goka – a family member whose names are both a female and male god to others – were mentioned and became a saviour.

CHAPTER 2

Understanding the gods

Philadelphia, PA, USA. October 17, 2017

The seventeen young women who came back with the Melon Elembele family men, whom they reciprocally admired, didn't cease any day, and for three months asked their husbands-to-be to ask Golu Goka as to understanding of gods, especially their village gods so named. They did so until the morning of the day they were to be adopted as members of the family, and he, Golu Goka, sat with them, the women, in two semicircles in front of him.

He first asked of the women's individual names – not that he had not met them at different times and called each by name – because that day was to be their special day: the adoption into a family and then a marriage to the respective seventeen men. They hastened to mention their names. And all seventeen mentioned their individual name at the same time, thus no name was heard but a chorus of names. Golu Goka then said a chorus and every chorus can only be part of only one song, but not of many songs, and therefore all seventeen would be adopted as one person and be given only one husband. There was silence by the seventeen women. Then, as if on a cue by an unheard and unseen person to them, the one whose name bore an alphabet earlier than the others mentioned her name: Alena. The second mentioned was Bartuna. The third, Clintona. The fourth, Darin. The fifth, Fiona. Other names called by a 'bearer' were Gena, Gera, Henam and Inia. The eight remaining mentioned Mirr, Noria, Notain, Orion, Pur, Zela, Zera, and Zetumta. "And to each name, each of you shall add the name 'Melon Elembele'," Golu Goka said. "And sisters, the night belongs to you. Each, and the man who nearly died for you because of reciprocal love, admiration, and the attention thereby, and therefore the chat in that village (your village). And even the daylight hours belong to you," Golu Goka advised.

They were about to rush away, each to look for her husband for a first night of togetherness (but not sexual health celebration or sharing), when Zetumta said, "We have not yet understood what our village gods, female Golu and male Goka, did that night in the village to save from death."

"Oh! Zetumta, your desire to understand how gods or goddesses save will make you avoid death always if you but listen attentively. When you call the right god's name or, in your village's case, a god and goddess's names, they will intervene in your situation whether their names were called by mere coincidence or whether you are an adherent or disciple or worshipper. My names are Golu Goka. It was only coincidental that they were the two names of your female and male gods.

"And the condemned men in calling my names, called a god and goddess names, and hence their intervention. It was not my intervention. That must be the understanding of how gods operate. They come to the rescue or intervene on behalf of whoever calls on them. And now to your 'twosome' nests, leaving gods behind but going with other gods or goddesses," Golu Goka advised.

CHAPTER 3

Zetumta tells the thoughts on her mind to Golu Goka and Melon Elembele Jnr

Philadelphia, PA, USA. October 18, 2017

When Zetumta arrived alone at the Melon Elembele Ideas Island's guest wing, the brothers Golu Goka and Melon Elembele Jnr were terrified that she had a story to tell of her marriage falling apart, because not once in the five years of marriage had she taken a journey alone, more so to the Ideas Island, where couples came for enrichment ideas each year for the subsequent year. But the two hoped for the best. And her first words were, "The gods give direction through instructions to solve emerging challenges when asked." And when she said those words, the two brothers sat straight and looked at each other as to whether they were failing, but made no attempt to say anything to question her, because Granddad Melon had taught them that the wise wait to hear till the end what a speaker wishes to say so as not to trigger a war of words and dissension in a family when another begins a journey of speaking. For however long, every journey ends, especially the journey of speaking when the speaker must break to take breaths.

"My two weeks, nights ago, were as if the night owls decided not to give me the rest of sleep but the torment of questions, my answers, their repudiation of my answers, and my further answers and their rejection by them, until I told them that I will make a search to find the correct answers. I got out of bed every night of those two weeks. And my husband didn't know of my getting up or the many thoughts of my head. I heard the words, '37 million of the female members of our family are not married'. I then knew that it was Mawu Sopkolisa who sent the night owls figuratively to bombard me with thoughts and to seek a solution. For there be some humans that are not gods, but the gods use them like gods because they call on the right gods to intervene to solve a pending or an arising challenge. Golu Goka was used in my then village, though he was no god, and the seventeen men called the gods' right names and were saved from death.

"I reasoned then that if there be 37 million unmarried sisters in our family alone, then if that number is multiplied by the number of families on Earth, the total would be four billion forty-eight million unmarried women. The gods have a challenge on their hands. And somebody must call on a god or a goddess to intervene and provide a solution. Oh, next I now recollect that as the owls of the night bombarded me, they put many thoughts in my head, such as: he that rules over five cities well will have added another five cities to rule making ten cities. And he that rules over two cities well, shall have added two more cities to rule over. Another was like this: he that invests his five talents well and earns another five talents will be commended.

"And he that invests his two talents well and earns two more talents will also be commended. But he that hides his one talent, will not be commended. His hidden talent will be taken away and given to him that had more. Could women be referred to as cities and or talents? That was my understanding.

"Another thought on my brain that night was: going in the strength of a particular 'food' for many days. And on this my mind was drawn to the Prophet Elijah who was said to have eaten bread baked on stones and drank water and went in the strength of that food, forty days. I am no Elijah. But Mawu Sokpolisa of Scripture makes prophets and prophetesses to hear and understand and tell humans Mawu Sokpolisa's word offering solutions. The night also reminded me of personal experiences. My three days of orgasmic experiences through a man – a husband – every month gave me strength and smiles the whole month. And I bubbled with awesome energy with no fleeting thought of any evil or fear but for those denied those orgasmic experiences who would not know God's awesome treat for fulsome living engendering goodness in women and men.

"The last thought of the last night of those two weeks in the last few hours before I got up was: there is a time for everything under the sun. And no one must miss any of those times or seasons. For God made them for human good. And missing any distorts your persona and makes you a different persona to serve not Mawu Sokpolisa.

"I have met the seventeen women, and not told them of the things I have told you. And I asked them if they would, if Mawu Sokpolisa wants them to bear with those who lack and share their husbands with at least nine others, if they will put themselves in those unmarried women's shoes as if the married were unmarried. Their answer so far has been a deep 'hmmm' of refusal. But the question is, why not? But – and now I am thinking aloud – if men or women call or cry out to gods or Mawu Sokpolisa to intervene by sending an equal number of men as the number of unmarried women I have mentioned – would that be possible? And my knowing that the men will come as boys and grow up into men – will that not solve the existing challenge of more women than men?"

"Give us days and nights unnumbered for the matter is tough?" both Golu Goka Elembele and Melon Elembele Jnr asked.

"It is the gods who make the laws and commands and can alter the laws and commands when called upon. Call upon our . . ." Zetumta mentioned no name, but added, "and I will share the joy endowed me through a relationship with a man with another woman till it is the turn of men to also share with nine other men 'one woman' in sexual health celebration or sharing."

9

CHAPTER 4

Seventeen fig trees with ten fruits on each

Philadelphia, PA, USA. October 19, 2017

When the seventeen women got to the wooded forest alone (without their husbands or brothers since they belonged to the same family either through birth or, in the case of the seventeen, through the process of adoption) they only expected to walk along, sweat a bit, and be chatty, but not to expect anything unusual. And especially for Zetumta, she was not expecting an answer to the things that were on her mind. On their walk, they spoke about their new ways of doing things in the Melon Elembele family, such as the creative ability by each person to add something new to what had been handed to him or her, and understanding or interpreting and utilizing things in nature for betterment of the family. The brain and hands were and are put to work every day, and what is seen as recreational or is recreational must enhance or give benefits to the family. Each woman was, therefore, on the lookout for the ordinary, mundane things, like water dripping from a leaf and dropping in the hair, or the dry brown leaves with insect pores on them falling among other brown leaves without insect pores. (Such are not noticed by many men and women of non-redeemed families who walk on Earth through its diverse mazes. These ones do not learn anything new because the nation has taken their power away from them.)

The first two miles of the walk yielded beauty of all hues that wooded areas offer, that urge you to want to see more by walking further till limbs and breath say, 'Another day, for we are unable to go further.'

At the third mile, by a tree-designated mark, a coconut fell but didn't hit the head of anyone, and it made them all look upwards. Then they asked among themselves as to why their looking had been forwards, horizontally, but not directly to the ground, or upwards, or sideways to the left or right, or alternating between all the listed. They took a decision for each three of them to use their eyes, ears and sense of feeling in a different direction from others for wider knowledge-gathering. And the last two, to record different sounds they would hear and what could have made the sound, so as to discuss at the day's end before retiring each to a husband's warm arms. And with no technological distraction to retard their progress through stopping to send or receive messages, or walking on with concentration on phones or tablets and missing markers, they continued to walk within the woods.

Zetumta spoke of smelling the aroma of the fruit of a fig tree in the distance, and her nose couldn't a mistake make. As to the direction and distance, she mentioned that it could only be the wind direction, as the nose knows not east, west, north or south cardinal directions, unlike the eye. (But with the eye's help, the nose could say that with certainty at times.) The wind direction was from north to south, and she could yet determine the distance, knowing that the closer to the fig tree, the more pronounced the smell picked by the nose.

After another quarter-mile walk, Zetumta loudly said that the eye could see the fig trees as the nose determined the ripeness of the fig tree's fruit – a hundred percent ripe – and when not plucked by humans and eaten, would naturally fall to the ground as food for the insects on ground, or attract flies of the sky who forage on the rottenness on the ground, denying the ground some nutrients.

A further walk of hundred yards and Darian spoke, asking who said the fig trees are in one location as if they are sisters and not wanting to live apart from each other. And to her statement, Zetumta explained that because they don't grow tall, they live apart from the tall trees so that they can also have sunlight. And on again came Darian, who said she had counted seventeen fig trees just as their number. "And to each of us, Mawu Sokpolisa has granted a present," she concluded.

Pur, who had been quiet most of the time on the walk, said, "The gods Golu and Goka from the village wish to give us a treat of fig fruits so that we will not forget where we came from, to always remember our roots, and if possible return to our village from time to time. For marriage must not make us forgetful of the land of our birth, but only to forget what our parents gave us so that we don't make comparisons between the present and the past." To her statement, Gera explained that they have more than a marriage – they have a new family by adoption, and have no home again in another land, the village, but the new home with new visions.

Zetumta explained that the number of fruits on each fig tree may be a confirmation of the direction that women must take to live long or forever.

"And what is that?" Fiona asked.

"What we do next is what will confirm the dream that gave the direction. Furthermore, if our husbands should arrive when we are next to the fig tree and behave in a particular way, then the gods or Mawu Sokpolisa have (has) given the new direction and confirmed it," Zetumta said.

"I need a fruit at this time to eat, whether washed or unwashed. Oh! While the fruit is hanging on the tree, nature through the rain and sunlight washes it of every bacterium, and the ground is wet in this location of the wooded area and the sun rays are directed at the tree, and so whoever wishes to eat along with me can eat," Alena said.

As each took a fruit to eat, they heard horses' hooves in the distance. And halfway through eating the fruit, their husbands or brothers dismounted, looking hungry and weary as if they had ridden hundreds of miles in search for a treasure trove – women – and they each plucked the remaining nine fruits on each of the seventeen trees.

At that, Zetumta said, "Golu Goka and Melon Elembele Jnr will, when told of what our husbands have done, decree that all male family members, for example, of the Elembele family, have ten women or sisters to a brother or a husband."

"We know why. And we are not averse to it at this time. It is of the gods' doing, or Mawu Sokpolisa's. And when they change, we comply with their change. None must suffer ill health or death by the denial of Mawu Sokpolisa's given rights to some by manmade rules," they all said as rote.

"It is the seventeen fig trees and their ten fruits each that spoke and confirmed what our Granddad Melon Elembele desired and wanted confirmation of to introduce but couldn't. We carry his mantle and introduce it until Mawu Sokpolisa decrees and confirms otherwise," their brothers or husbands said, while each galloped away on his horse with the wife.

CHAPTER 5

The plagues didn't touch the Melon Elembele family

Philadelphia, PA, USA. October 20, 2017

'The Melon Elembele Curse' was one headline in the newspaper with worldwide circulation. The only cable network read its version on air of, 'The biggest family has its own god, but not God, the universal God', and said, 'The Melon Elembele's end has come as it seeks to promote marriage between siblings, but one brother to uncountable sisters. Well, sexual relations are what the family values. Sex is its god. No doubt their Granddad Melon Elembele married many women, and did it in secret. But his successors are doing in the open, in grander ways. No woman should be denied sexual relations because it is a God-ordained right. But where is the equality of the sexes? When a man can have a number of women as sexual partners, but women cannot have many sexual partners? That is discrimination. Their women must rise against their brothers, their husbands. We must put them all to death if their leaders will not reverse this curse-attracting decision.'

Every five minutes, the mocking words were repeated on air by radio, social media or the cable networks.

The Melon Elembele family networks didn't as much as try to deny that it had issued instructions to that effect. But stated that all family members should and must stand firm to do what was and is prudent and right to do in an era of dishonesty, of false scales, or weights and measures.

On the first night of the new measures taking place of a brother (husband) having many wives, with the first sister taking her showers and to be followed by the brother or husband, lightning struck in every Melon Elembele man's home, splitting the electrical bulb switch in the bathroom and turning the bathroom into total darkness. The brother was therefore forced to go into the bathroom with an emergency torch, which he shone as the woman took her bath. After her, he also did. Then, there arose a bright light in the bathroom, making the torchlight unnecessary. The brother and the woman (or sister) walked hand in hand into the bedroom. And romance only fit for the gods commenced with endearing words as to the woman (or sister's) splendour and virgin- womanliness unexplored, while she spoke of his masculinity and ruggedness to protect her – not as a mauling tiger, but to cover her with the warmth of the protective cloth of romance. He kissed her. And a trumpet sounded as she returned that kiss, the first in thirty-five years.

They continued, and went to the second stage of their touching each other with hugs and the language of 'mmm' and 'ah' understood by the gods and that accompany sexual health passion to make it a celebration to be remembered. As she crouched on the floor, reeling from her first time of sexual health pleasure with multiple orgasms, she expressed that only Mawu Sokpolisa must be praised and honoured. While he also gave vent to words of praise and honour to Mawu Sokpolisa.

He stooped, lifted her from the floor and onto the bed, and assured her that every hour till dawn she would express unspeakable joy through tears when they were linked together and wished to have the arrears of sexual health pleasure restored to her. And seven times that night, she hallowed Mawu Sokpolisa, after every hour.

When, at breakfast that morning, she said the prayer over the breakfast of four-course meals, she asked also that she be allowed to say the post-breakfast prayer. She did, saying, "You get closer to Mawu Sokpolisa through earthly marriage and enjoy its sweetness through sexual health celebration, and that confirms to you that the practical wow of Earth's marriage is a foretaste of Mawu Sokpolisa's three times over, and that is why it is referred to as 'heaven'."

And so that was a first night for this sister (wife) and many sisters (wives) in the Melon Elembele family. And with joy and gladness on the faces and hearts of these women first-timers, their prayers and songs resounded to Mawu Sopkolisa, who felt proud and gave great working ideas to the Melon Elembele family.

New gadgets and inventions came out the day following the night of love and sexual health passion. But while the Melon Elembele members were celebrating the new gadgets and inventions, a plague, the first of boils, appeared on the lips, noses, both eyes, in both palms, on the navels, in the pubic regions, in their sexual organs or on them, the knee caps and the soles of the feet of men and women of the people of the nations in the various countries of the world.

In their moment of intense pain and suffering, they cursed the Melon Elembele family members for bringing the curses of the gods on them. But they wondered why the accursed were moving about in their vehicles, aircrafts and whatever they were moving about in with gaiety on the faces, while most of them were bedridden or at hospitals receiving treatment. And as the day drew to a close – in some countries and later in other countries depending on the time zones – the Melon Elembele family brothers or husbands prepared to welcome other sisters or wives to their first time of knowing themselves sexually as women, and understanding brothers (husbands) as men and the differences. They also came to know why Mawu Sokpolisa made two distinct genders, and why Mawu Sokpolisa desired a marital relationship with the two sexes other than any other form of relationship.

The second night was for women bearing the name Darian and names starting with the alphabet letter D. There were seven million women of the Melon Elembele family available with a name starting with D that night to meet with their brothers or husbands. In homes, the brothers (husbands) cooked in anticipation of the arrival of the sisters or wives who had never had sexual health sharing or celebration throughout their teenage years till this night of expectation.

They were all in the forty-year bracket, having kept their chastity – unlike women of the people of nations or non-family-matched women who regularly used tools or their own hands to trigger such passions, but deny that they have had any sexual acts. And well, most of them were right, for they didn't perform the acts with men and therefore felt Mawu Sokpolisa should not fault them. When the hour struck 7pm across locations with Melon Elembele family members, those who were to have their first sexual health celebration or sharing with their brothers (husbands) ate a light meal with the husbands. Thereafter, those who didn't shower before the evening meal took their showers, and these turned out to be husbands for the sisters (wives) who had showered and perfumed their bodies in anticipation.

At 9pm, it was as if the god of romance, who sends waves of passions, had sent perfumed wind over each 'couple' as lips touched lips in kissing, and arms and legs rubbed against each other, as words to electrify their bodies were spoken out – the untutored wives, without the learnt language of romance, spoke through spirits. With one act behind them, and its orgasm showing through the shaking of the body, these wives knelt down to thank Mawu Sokpolisa, and expressed that more gratitude they would offer as many as seven times that night in appreciation that Mawu Sokpolisa had granted permission for them to partake of the awesome goodness of sexual health celebration or sharing.

And their expectation was not denied them. Unlike the first set of couples, who did not sing as the morning hours broke in adoration to Mawu Sokpolisa a song, these second sets sung a song: 1: 'Joy wells in us. A heart touched. A body touched. Waves triggered. A pleasure released. And released, again and again. Mawu Sokpolisa, your praise we utter. For excellent are your gifts. We will bow in honour many times. For great are your works. And greater the subsequent days.' And 2: 'Hmm! Mawu Sokpolisa! You have given us a smile and laughter. No frowns will show on our faces again. Mawu Sokpolisa, our promise. The night was awesome. Mawu Sokpolisa made it that way. And so that the day's work of our hands will be excellent. And we will bless you with our first fruits and offerings.'

When the rays of the sun shone in their various bedrooms, and they each started stepping out for that day's work, the smiles and laughter were as long as the Atlantic Ocean and enough for any employer to expect productivity to rise threefold. And it did rise that day for the various Melon Elembele industries and firms.

And while they were counting their good fortune, the people of the nations in the various countries of the world were mourning the deaths of many, as husbands killed many millions of wives because the boils on their bodies had healed, but those within had not healed and they refused to yield to their husbands' demands. Their husbands, therefore, sought for sexual pleasure with robots. While the unmarried continued seeking satisfaction through introduction or insertion of select types of fruits and gadgets improvised for such.

When it was the turn of day three, or rather night three, the sisters (wives) went for the things of night, some of them, and four million of them out of six million sought to tie their expectation of what would happen in the bedrooms, or elsewhere, and later ending on beds, through the questioning of the night one and night two wives. But they refused to tell them anything of how the night progressed with the brothers (husbands.) They rather advised them to be expectant, open up, give or yield up their bodies and be active participants to receive and to give. For one person cannot give sexual health celebration to envelope two. It is for two active persons.

Philadelphia, PA, USA. October 21, 2017

When it was time for the fourth, fifth and six batch of sisters (wives – the untouched) to take their turn on their respective days, they, also numbering millions, took a day's fast and prayed to Mawu Sokpolisa to grant them momentous pleasures as they celebrated a time or times of the first sexual health celebration.

They asked Mawu Sokpolisa (the five-names-god and the ruler and giver of all things beautiful, pure and hallowed) to accept the anticipated and expected wondrous time of sexual health celebration and related orgasmic shakes as a sacrifice, sweet-smelling and pleasing to Mawu Sokpolisa, and grant them children to nurture and for only goodness to reign on Earth.

And as each batch did the seven per night sexual health celebration, they got out of bed with the strength of teenagers, though in their mid-forties. Then came to pass in their words, "Our strength is renewed like the eagles and will continue to be renewed every day as the night offers us the awesome pleasures, the benefits of unrestrained sexual health celebration. Praise we all our Mawu Sokpolisa with heart and voices at night and day." And they also said, "We have discovered the shadow state of heaven. We will live in it because we now know what heaven entails – pure and restrained love – and when matched with prayer at the end of each sexual health celebration, releases heavenly ideas making Earth heavenly."

As they left the bedrooms for the routine activities of the daylight hours, they felt light, and bubbled with energy and laughter, and smiles were on every face radiating glorious light without the need for the sun's light.

Darkness those six days was the lot of the people of the nations in the various countries of the world, and a thick blanket of sorrow covered them because of their self-arrogated sexual acts and waywardness. Many of them, because of their depressive state, became lunatics and roamed the streets unclothed. A plague of paralysis descended on some also, and then their leaders asked: 'Do the Melon Elembeles have a new god? Are they right in what they are doing? And we are wrong? Who are our gods? And why are they unlike the Melon Elembele gods to bless and to prosper us, but are destroying us as if we are wrong?' With no one to answer their questions – not that they sought a member of the Melon Elembele family to put the question to him or her – their questions remained an answered.

With only few million of the Melon Elembele family sisters (wives) to go for the first time, and have the benefit of sexual health celebration, those who had tasted of Mawu Sokpolisa's goodness in endowing men and women with the sexual organs to rejuvenate the body, organized a six-hour festival of praise across countries where the Melon Elembeles lived. They sang songs like angels, for there were no wrong notes sung in any song. As the festival was ending, the song leaders shouted, "When you carry out Mawu Sokpolisa's will or changed will upon plea, you become a beloved child to enjoy all of Mawu Sokpolisa's pleasures for evermore. And your revilers, who do their own will, suffer defeat and destruction every new day for they are not protected by a god."

At her words, the millions echoed three times the names, 'Mawu Sokpolisa'.

When the three remaining batches of Melon Elembele family sisters (wives) had taken their turn and thus the thirty-seven million women or sisters had equality with other members of the family, then it was that Golu Goka Elembele and Melon Elembele Jnr both declared that: "We are truly one family under one god, Mawu Sokpolisa, none wayward, carrying on Mawu Sokpolisa's will, and no plague attaches to us because our god is a god of order and we are of order."

And as further plagues affected the people of the nations in the various countries of the world, this final time through the invasion of mosquitoes in their homes and diverse kinds of reptiles attacking and killing or poisoning them, the only elder left of the people of the nations said, "It is because their god, the Melon Elembele family's god, is a god of sexual health love, and celebrating sexual health amounts to a sacrifice to it, and because the Melon Elembele family celebrated so excellently and exceptionally, their god prospered them with wealth and wellbeing. And while our god of the people of the nations in the various countries of the world detests sexual acts by anyone, Melon Elembele sexual health celebration brought curses on us, because they lived among us and annoyed our god with their sexual health celebrations on Earth."

But he quickly retracted and said, "No, their god, the Melon Elembele family god, is a god of order, and members of that family were, and are, persons of order. Gods want obedience to orders. We lacked obedience and didn't know the orders of our god, hence the plagues attaching to us. I will lead the 'plagued' remaining people of the nations in the various countries of the world to seek the names and attributes of the Melon Elembele family god and worship it. Ah! I have heard it being called 'Mawu Sokpolisa'."

CHAPTER 6

Nine babies, nine new mothers, one father

Philadelphia, PA, USA. October 22, 2017

When nine months were ended, from those nine days of sexual health festival, each day for nine days, then was heard the first cry of a baby, the happy holding of baby to a mother's chest, the joy of motherhood, the nurturing of life through breastfeeding many times a day, unashamed that others would see lactating breasts – not that they are not of spellbound attraction to non-baby males, but their unavailability then for some roles. Nine mothers in a home cuddling each a baby for six months or more months, away from non-home work schedules, with growth spurts attracted the gods of health and wellbeing to stay in the home, for sickness and disease to stay out outside its doors and not to enter when a mother is for an hour away doing the things of womanhood and not motherhood then. And so, in nine days, 37 million babies and voices and all of them with the Melon Elembele name carried, and there was the widening and spread of one family as more and more of the people of the nations in the countries of the world were dying in multiples but with no new births, possibly a punishment of the gods and goddesses of fertility and birth, not to visit them again.

With pride and continued joy that they had also produced a kindred spirit, these 37 million Melon Elembele wives or sisters set a day aside to connect by phone creating a loop of thirty-seven million mouths to shout aloud the words, "I have added virtue to the world by the birth, and not subtracted what Granddad Melon Elembele left behind. We are the light of the world and nothing can restrain light."

On the last day of the thirteenth month, the loop was made across different time zones and climates, but with the same words spoken. And when that was done, other spirit beings other than gods were released by the gods to minister around the clock to the new mothers and their growing babies, incidentally all of them girls. And at the festival of a woman's first child's 'open womb' anniversary, these mothers (37 million) three months pregnant again, unlike other Melon Elembele family women, linked by simultaneous phone calls, said: "We celebrate, dear daughters. You will grow in love and share love of the Melon Elembele's day or night, winter or summer. And don't block the womb for others to be birthed so that one day only Melon Elembeles will inhabit Earth, for Earth's paradise to be established like heaven's. Mawu Sokpolisa, your plans will be fulfilled."

When the statement ended, they all retired to cut a melon of diverse types and distributed them to all in each Melon Elembele home to eat, while mothers blended the melons for their babies.

At night that same day, Anna and Melon Elembele Jnr in the privacy of their home, as the successors to Granddad Melon Elembele, put out all lights and put it on again and declared that: "In darkness or in light, only the Melon Elembele light remains as the light of the world, for its light derives from Mawu Sokpolisa." A dinner of herbs was then eaten by them, and when the night wore on, their bodies joined in sexual health celebration as a sacrificial offering to Mawu Sokpolisa, who was well pleased with such.

CHAPTER 7

The Melon Elembele family five-senses-war arsenal

Philadelphia, PA. USA. October 23, 2017

Granddad Melon Elembele didn't ever hold a gun or make any of us to dream of owning a gun or using the mind to create any tool that could be used to main or kill another. His belief was that Mawù Sokpolisa, who brought to birth, was capable of securing humans in Mawu Sokpolisa's will from gods or goddesses' attack on Earth. And for humans as against humans, if you are not misled, do not move out from your home of protection and security to a place for another's at the wrong time. Your five senses were and are capable of protecting and securing you from harm or threat or destruction. He taught us that the better weapons for harm, threat or destruction were the mouth for speech, the eyes for sight, the ears for hearing, the nose to breathe or for breathing, and the sense of feel or touch. Not ever in his lifetime were these senses deployed as instruments of war, because we were not ever under harm's way, threat or destruction. But recently, when the men and women of the people of the nations in the various countries of the world were dying, they planned to kill us as ransom to their gods or goddesses so that they may no more die, and by our death, they will remain living beings. And so, the instruction went from Anna and Melon Elembele Jnr reminding us of the weapons of warfare to use to prevent our substitutionary deaths.

It then dawned on us that the things given to us – the five senses for human survival, the weapons for defence or protection – could or would also be used for attacking when you know how to use them for attack. And that use or those uses, Granddad Melon Elembele taught each infant while still an infant how to use, but not on Melon Elembele family member or members. Not one member has used or remembered to use any of these weapons against family.

And when we knew the day for the first attack was on us, we spoke loudly and the ears of our enemies, the people of nations in the various countries of the world, were unable to hear, and when their commanders spoke, none heard and none moved. They stood still wherever they were as we moved through and fro our day's activities.

The commanders, shocked and disappointed that none moved because their ears were all gone deaf, planned the next attack of destruction against us. We pre-emptively laughed all through the night before the daylight hours for the attack, and their tongues crept to their mouths and no one among them could speak, not even use signs. Stunned and lost for words, because they (the people of the nations in the various countries of the world) couldn't express themselves in words, they drew back, thinking we were not men or women but gods and goddesses who knew and used pre-emptive war tactics.

Next, they waited a three-day wait before setting out to invade our homes and to destroy us by death, and they only to live on Earth. When we discerned that motive, we pre-emptively made flesh fill their eardrums and they became unbalanced, unable to stand or walk anywhere to cause destruction. And they became and walked like four-footed animals. Afraid that they would crawl on all fours to attack us, we sent a pungent smell into their nostrils that took away their sense of smell from them. Thus, they couldn't smell and know of our existence on Earth since it is only living things that give off smell (aroma). The fifth weapon we pre-emptively unleashed on them, (remembering that our god, Mawu Sokpolisa, is the five-names god), was the removal or the taking away of the sense of feeling, and that done, flies, insects and worms stung, sucked or ate them, and their remains that the

25

insects couldn't eat or didn't eat became part of the earth as manure and our crops grew well as a result.

And we celebrated the goodness of Mawu Sokpolisa, whose weapons were the best.

And we had peace in the land for there lived no one a lawbreaker, or one who didn't ask permission of Mawu Sokpolisa but did as he thought right in his own mind. We rejoiced many nights after all these things or events because we shed not the blood of anyone to offend Mawu Sokpolisa, who detested seeing the blood or the picking of the smell of blood. And there will be our destruction also by Mawu Sokpolisa, leaving Earth uninhabited.

The Earth remains Melon Elembele's, with only the five-senses-war arsenal.

CHAPTER 8

The children of rain

Philadelphia, PA, USA. October 24, 2017

"The night is not long or longer than any other, but if you don't sleep at night and you are not occupied with anything to occupy your mind and time, the night will be long. The night to an unrequited lover is longer than all, because restful sleep that makes the clock that ticks fast and un-knowningly, takes you to the next dawn of waking up to start another day of work, does not avail to him or her," Melon Elembele Jnr explained to sisters who gave birth to children for the first time in the previous two years, and some of whom (as they have to come in batches) had arrived in his home for a visit to learn the ropes of nurturing from Anna.

"Your introduction to the topic you mentioned for after supper time chat has no relevance," Zetumta said.

"Oh! It is to emphasize the importance of storytelling at night to your children for a restful night's sleep. The excitement associated with the storyline determines the level of sleep for that refreshing sleep. And the storyline should not end at a point that makes their minds to begin a search throughout the night for what did not happen, did happen, or will not happen. The end of the story must put their minds at ease. And therefore, storytelling at night prior to falling asleep must be a learned art. Anna will tell you a story that teaches," Melon Elembele Jnr said.

"Bedtime stories to children are simply to induce sound sleep and trigger good memory when the child rises from sleep at the cock crowing (these days they don't, as they don't live within human habitation)," Anna said. "Where have all the cocks gone? Ah! To the outskirts of cities and towns, far from human habitation, and we are losing the benefit of their capacity to tell time and warn of upcoming dangers, say the death of some, and what preventive measures to take to avert their warnings, when those who understand the cocks' warnings hear them issue the warnings, or the rustling brown leaves with a remembrance of the story. One day, if not on this trip, I will tell you how by not living in homes with animals, we have lost the lessons they teach us that maybe forewarnings, or how to do certain things, like rising up and walking in your compound or courtyard to derive the benefit of the dew of dawn or the morning—"

Zetumta interrupted her to say, "Wake up so early and also children?"

"When a people forsake what their grandfathers and grandmothers did with regard and respect for nature, disequilibrium sets in and nature stops conferring some benefits on them and they are the worse for it. Humans, therefore, are the losers. The story of the children of rain falls into the realm of nature. Listen attentively till the end, and you will always do the things that the children of rain desire so as to get reciprocal benefit.

"How do we get rain on Earth? When we go out into the open spaces and dance either under the moonlit nights or in the afternoons of some days, as the excitement grows and we are vigorously dancing to the drum beat and music that attracts the attention of some of children of rain to come out from their homes above in the skies and dance. And as they dance more vigorously, they begin to sweat and their sweat begins to the fall to ground, and the intensity of the rains is equivalent to the intensity or the vigorousness of their dancing and also equal to their sweat drops. And in an area where the children and adults alike don't dance to drums and songs, the children of rain are not attracted to come out of their homes to also dance, triggering their body sweat to fall as rain. Hmm! The children of rain are what are called nature water beings or spirit beings—"

Zetumta spoke again without allowing Anna to complete her sentence, saying, "Eh! Then the hurricanes that bring rain and winds, strong winds to cause destruction, numbered from one to five, come to destroy because the children of rain, and the adults in rain's household, join hands with the children of wind and possibly adults in the household of rain to cause the devastation."

"Ah! Zetumta, you have got it all mixed up, but intelligently brought in the children of wind and the adults in wind's household. There are five human levels on Earth. Five levels in the rain world. And, as you have rightly brought up, five levels in the wind world and five levels in the sun world.

"The levels were determined through age brackets or groupings at the time everything came into existence. They are: children as the Sion group; teenagers, they are the Bonan group; adults are the Rithan group; the elderly, the Votune group; and the last group, are the Ifan group, that is the elderly, infirm or weak who use their last strength before death, 'dying strength' or 'power' it is called, a power unparalleled by any of the other four groups' powers.

"When the Ifan group notices offence on Earth, they are not triggered by any group of dancers or singers or music on Earth to go out profusely sweating to enlist the services of a like group among wind's household, or rain's household, or sun's household to cause devastation on Earth.

"What causes rain to fall for the crops to grow or the trees to be watered and look luxuriantly green also causes havoc. The reason behind the negative destruction, is because the rain, its children and adults, the wind, its children and adults, and the sun with its children and adults, are respectively God's, and gods and goddesses to give good and lifegiving things, and also bad or destructive things or life destruction things, when their wills we disobey," Anna concluded.

Fiona asked, "Can there be sound, restful sleep when such is told as a bedtime story?"

"When good and obedient people live on Earth, nothing destructive ever occurs to them. Theirs are always good things, and every story that has a good end is a bedtime story," Anna answered.

"Ah-hah! The Melon Elembele's stories all have good endings and are the only bedtime stories fit for all the groups, even the Sion group. The Melon Elembele children have always pleased the children of rain, the children of wind, the children of the sun, and not one ever was or will be destroyed," Zetumta concluded.

CHAPTER 9

The animals offer us protection

Philadelphia, PA, USA. October 24, 2017

"My dear, have you taken a good look at yourself of late? Looks can reveal or do reveal a lot about us. And even about other living things in nature, that is on land, under the vast expanse of waters, and in the skies or the heavenlies," Anna said after dinner one night when they were on the sailing watercraft.

"I was afraid to say it. I have been troubled many years. The thought of saying that human beings look like diverse animals was troubling, when that day we changed into at least two thousand different animals, I was troubled by the thought of change and the change itself, and the fear that if we didn't change into a human form again, and what would have happened to us. Two thousand humans remaining animals and changing their habitation from homes into a forest, to be beaten by the rains or the sunshine or stung by insects, made me hope that if it did ever happen again, I would specify a timeline to live like an animal and therefore be in charge of my destiny and not leave it to chance. And even in doing that, just for the purpose of having a different experience, that of using the mind of animal and reasoning as an animal," Melon Jnr explained.

"Hmm. Are sure about all that you have said? Of using the mind of an animal and reasoning like an animal? Then you should not have spoken about the fear, if that day, we didn't change back into human form. Alternatively, maybe you had the fear because you were not in control, and on that I cannot fault you. I am aware that every human looks like one animal. And I will hasten to say that with regard to trees and even humans have a resemblance to fishes of the sea. And my husband, what animal do you look like? And would you want to live like that animal for one day? I will grant your request–"

Melon interrupted her and said, "Not that fast."

"Eh, you have failed me this time. You said what you didn't mean. If you won't change as the leader of the family, I would change again and again, and there would be no opportunity for you to be near me in the forest. Tigers and the wolves will eat you up. And I would be a hungry one. You said too much. Maybe the wine 'opened' your mouth too wide without the corresponding courage. Well, this evening, I only sought from you to know what animal it was that I look like. And what animal you look like," Anna said.

"You must see yourself as looking like one or two of our friends of the wild before saying that about another human being, more so a wife. I need to look in the mirror for hours. And take a careful look at those animals of the wild and make an informed decision. Photos or pictures might not give a good resemblance. At least those humans with whiskers may mention some two or three animals quickly as their lookalikes, but not me, as I wear no beard or whiskers," Melon Jnr explained.

"Then you have time granted you by me to do a search many times over. But today, I am repeating that every human, none excluded, resembles one animal or other through facial expressions or attitudes. Our family from generations therefore didn't lord it (with pride) over them, and they made themselves available to serve us. I don't speak about cats or dogs or domestic animals as pets. I speak about those in the real world of wild. Let no fear enter your heart and mind to think of our using sorcery on the animals. You have been part of our family and have been its foremost head for twenty-plus years, going into thirty. I hope you have heard the roars or other animal sounds as you slept in various family properties across the countries. They keep watch over us; actually, they are our foremost security that ensures our indestructibility and invisibility, because our protectors were and are invisible, though seen by eyes, but we are not seen. The animals are seen by the people of the nations in the countries of the world. You have felt their movements, picked their scents with your nostrils, heard their sounds but not seen them with your power of sight. And if you don't know any one of the three things about our guardian animals, don't you worry. They are out there, above all Melon Elembele properties, and an outsider who notices sees a zoo with animals walking to and fro, or doing something else and fear (in the form of a spider's web), covers the person, and the person moves many miles away from our properties. And you can't break into our properties, the guardian animals will attack you," Anna explained in detail.

"Eh! All of sudden with my closed eyes, as if in sleep, I am seeing blue lights, showing the eyes of many cats. Have I not been spiritual enough to have noticed the things you spoke about this evening? My answer to my own question is that when a family has fool-proof or secure-proof security, it is impenetrable. And I am unworried in not knowing it all. The man Melon Elembele has been all things and everything. Because Mawu Sokpolisa was with him, giving directions or confirming things," Melon Elembele Jnr said, and tapped the wife who headed towards the bedroom.

CHAPTER 10

The people of the nation's launch a final onslaught

Philadelphia, PA, USA. October 25, 2017

Their gods were also blessing us. And all because their people individually said kind words about us. But our daily expansion remained a mystery to them. Anna wrote on the husband's letterhead that the leaders of the people of the nations in the various countries of the world had met at the countries' headquarters and took a decision that death to the Melon Elembele family would ensure the survival of the people of the nations in the various countries of the world. Their attack on the family was to be a surprise. And, therefore, the Melon Elembele must see every day not as their last day in the world, but a day to continue to do good to other humans and other living things for their gods and Mawu Sokpolisa, the god of all living things to fight for them.

Not two days after the dispatch of the letter, fires broke out around the malls in ninety countries, and the firefighters stood aghast as they had not seen before fires that stretched forty thousand feet up into the night sky and were seen in another sixty countries as if the fires were from a god of destruction. Unable to fight the fire, they only hoped that it would move horizontally rather than the vertical projection taken as they would be able to contain it.

"If there is a fire god in the universe, this must be its fire, not a human's," the lead fireman said.

The few gathered Melon Family members stood silently with each a leaf in his or her mouth so that words would not be heard from the lips, for their belief was that in any tragedy, words could be spoken wrongly and offend a god who would otherwise have helped.

An armoured squadron came later in addition to police, emergency services, just in case people decided to loot; but as the fire was raging, they saw a woman walk from the mall towards the east; another woman walked out from the mall through the raging fire towards the north; and both were not seen when television crews rushed to where they saw them walking to. Next came out a man, who looked the same age and like a brother of the first woman unto the western side of the mall, with his back turned to the blazing fire; another man with features like the second woman also came out, and both men, as if they communicated, flew upwards, and at that instant, torrential rains the size of the fires descended and quenched the fire.

Then someone was heard, saying, "The fire was the fire of protection that protected the owners, and such a fire under certain circumstances would be a fire of attack against the enemies of those who worship the god of the fire of protection. I have read about it in a book written by an Imoniian female author," he said.

While the lead fire officer, who recognized him, called him by name, "Tapita, do you believe most things written by authors? They are, most times, their crazy imaginations, unless they were inspired. Most of them, if not all, are either psychotics or the adherents of gods whom they don't question but believe whatever they say to them."

"Hmm! Officer," Tapita said, "have you seen the fire burn anything? Strange fires as those fires would be called and are caused by gods whose dwellings are not among humans, but when invoked act on behalf of some humans. Didn't you see the apparitions or real men and women? The two women and two men who came out through the raging fire signify that some are not subject to the power or strength of fires; but us, who seek to not learn to know more about the world of unconventional things. For whatever happens on Earth has its opposite. What I read about ten years ago, I have witnessed it today to ground my belief – not that I then didn't believe when I read.

"Your men and you will lose your jobs if the strange event that occurred, the torrential rains that quenched the fire, were to become the norm. If all humans could summon such rainfalls to also quench fires set by matches, gas leaks, or what not, nobody will need firemen or firewomen again. It will be humans losing jobs not to computers or robots that can be seen, but this time to spiritual robots or computers that cannot be seen but their end result. People remain fools when the unusual doesn't teach them newer knowledge for them to subscribe to the newer knowledge, and move on to accept the new things and do greater and better things."

When Tapita finished his 'one-sided discourse' he noticed that there were shoppers in the mall, but no harm came to any.

The leaders of the people of the nations in the various countries of the world met again and decided that the Melon Elembele brand was so interwoven with every stratum of humanity, that when you sought to destroy them, you were likely to destroy more of your own people than them.

Exactly a week to the day on which the first incident occurred, further plans were made to strike hard at the Melon Elembele residences in every country.

Anna and Melon Elembele Jnr, aware of the time that their enemies were to strike, but two hours before then, invoked the name of Mawu Sokpolisa to the following effect: "We stand at the threshold of our lives, whatever we stood for, even our belief and trust in you Mawu Sokpolisa, would come to an end, if we should perish. It would be your will to preserve us because we are your heritage. And your weapons are protective. And the same weapons are destructive. Two hours hence, who will do Mawu Sokpolisa's will when we are destroyed. In your hands we commit our safety. We have no fear."

Both went down on their knees, and turned through the four cardinal points, and loud were the rumblings. It was as if the heavens would break their bounds. But they ceased suddenly.

Then the oceans began the swift flow, taking down only houses of the people of the nations in the various countries of the world by encircling their homes with the rushing, gushing waters, while along Melon Elembele properties were formed walls of solid ice and not a drop of water entered any home of theirs. And just before dusk, that day, the corpses of the people of the nations in the various countries in the world were buried when the Earth opened and closed on them. Only a select few of the people of the nations in the countries of the world survived, so that they could have the opportunity to decide which way to go; to remain intransigent or follow after Mawu Sokpolisa who, through the Melon Elembele family, fed them with its stores of food and wealth. While and when the 'remnants' were contemplating why their actions were pre-empted with the destruction of most of the people of the nations in the various countries of the world, the Melon Elembeles stood on their knees for an hour and rose up to eat a sacrificial meal of roasted corn powder and broiled fish.

Some weeks after, the 'remnants' knocked for the first time on the doors of Melon Elembeles, seeking to know why they were not destroyed by the raging destructive sea waves but protected by the same waves that turned to walls of ice and formed bulwarks of protection for them.

"When we gave you from our malls and our farms every three years, for half a year, food to eat without payment and other things free, we had purchased your lives with our good deeds. And turning against us, to destroy us, our gods and your gods saw it as wickedness on your part and joined hands to destroy your people instead. Good people will have been destroyed and only evil people of the nations in the various countries of the world will have remained on Earth. Such will not be permitted by Mawu Sokpolisa and other gods, your gods and goddesses even," the Melon Elembele family answered.

"And will you continue to provide for us and our children so that we will not die of hunger?" the remaining people of the nations in the various countries of the world demanded to know.

"Our pact remains with gods, though the responsibilities are to human beings – the people of nations in the various countries of the world. The gods have done us no wrong for us to abrogate a pact with them. Not that it lies in our power but with our god, Mawu Sokpolisa," they, Melon Elembele family, answered.

"We will begin to serve you and your god, Mawu Sokpolisa, if only you will tell your god not to send the third and also the final weapons of defences and attacks – the wind – against us. For it is merciless when it attacks. It comes back with fire and water in its trail, leaving disorder and burning disorder, and there will be none to clear the disorder," the people of the nations in the various countries of the world said.

CHAPTER 11

When sexual health wellbeing begins

Philadelphia, PA, USA. October 26, 2017

A couple of months after the destruction of most of the people of the nations in the various countries of the world, and their inability to determine that there were one billion people of the nations in the countries of the world left, there arose one hundred self-appointed leaders who took it upon themselves to understand the past and its events so as to guarantee a future of hope and increases in its population and not further decreases. The first question they asked of us, the Melon Elembele, was why their gods of promiscuity didn't protect them from deaths though they as a people were excellent and exceptional in carrying out varied acts multiple times each day as a sacrifice to their gods, who should have rewarded them with bumper harvests of crops, fishes, and anything and everything that makes a nation wealthy and powerful. They also asked to know why when we married our family members, some of us, as many as ten, or as many women as we could provide a home for, the gods looked on us with favour and enlarged our wealth and wellbeing and even increased our population by adding at least a minimum of 37 million annually.

And our family response was: "There is sexual health wellbeing sharing between men and women in an ordered way by a god when the god gives instructions or commands as to what the people must do. Alternatively, the fathers of a family, or the people of the nations could, depending on the challenges faced by the family or the people of the nations, approach their god, in our case, Mawu Sokpolisa and seek for approval. In our case, approval was sought by the fathers or mothers, rightly called holy fathers or holy mothers, persons who had done or carried on the will of the Mawu Sokpolisa, without turning to the left or right, and had favour with Mawu Sokpolisa to alter the instructions or commands previously given to avoid reproach from their enemies in solving a challenge that had arisen since the prior instruction or command.

"There was always a leeway with gods and goddesses. And when we noticed that one of the two natural genders were disproportionate to the other, and they, after many, many years of waiting for partners to share sexual health wellbeing and not finding could or will do a wrong and bring reproach to Mawu Sokpolisa, by copying the ways of the people of the nations among whom they dwell, who were promiscuous without the semblance of any order, we sought for approval from Mawu Sokpolisa to do things as will be consistent with order or orderly. For the gods and goddesses themselves know that there was and is a time for doing everything on Earth and, when reminded that the time was passing by, will give an order, but not an order dictated by man. And we obtained approval instructed and confirmed by Mawu Sokpolisa, our god.

"While in your case, your gods or goddesses didn't have any say in what you did, we sought the approval of our god that bears five names. No woman of our family who shared sexual health wellbeing with a particular man in the family would have approached another man in our family to share sexual health wellbeing since we didn't seek approval for such. But yours was not a sharing of sexual health wellbeing between approved women and a man, or approved men and a woman if that was what you were granted permission or approval to do.

"In the way you acted, you overrode the laws, instructions and commands of your many gods or goddesses and made yourselves superior to them, and they turned and fought you or simply left you to fight spiritual battles that should not be fought by you, the people of the nations, by yourselves. That was why you lost, but we won.

"And one question you didn't ask, that you should have asked was, why the Melon Elembele charged only one percent as its profit over and above the price of goods and services or rents or fares, for example. Additionally, why every three years, we offered six months of goods or services without receiving any payment and did that again after three years. We sought not to take advantage of you and to make you penurious, converting you to slaves, human as you are. If we had done that, a god liberator would have heard your cry one day and would have dispossessed us of our slaves and our wealth and turned it over to the slaves. That is a lesson in nature, generally available to be made known to humans, but not known and understood by the rich or wealthy people of the people of the nations in the countries of the world to seek. And finally, in giving you things without price or cost, we purchase our lives from your gods also, and a ransom we will not ever be as sacrifice for others but they our ransom," the Melon Elembele family concluded.

"After all, we all can live harmoniously with all the gods, if always we take with us words to them. Sexual health wellbeing will begin at its timeline, other things at their timelines, for there is a time for everything on Earth," the leaders of the people of the nations in the countries of the world said, and suffered no more destruction for a period of time, their gods and goddesses hoping that they would behave from thence as the Melon Elembele family members.

CHAPTER 12

Whose value, mine or yours? Granddad Melon Elembele's example

Philadelphia, PA, USA. October 26, 2017

"Whether Granddad Melon was at the threshold of redeeming his family members many decades earlier, he met a teenager, so goes the story, who informed him that he had been sent with two round stones, perfectly round and each three inches in circumference by the seventy-year-old mother to give the two stones to Melon Elembele for a value that Melon Elembele should determine. And that was all the resources they, Mum and son, had and were living for. The teenager added that in whoever's hands were the stones determined their value.

Granddad Melon Elembele took the two stones, held one in each hand and closed his hand around each. The tighter or the stronger he closed his hands around the stones, the warmer each stone felt and therefore his hands. And also, the longer he held them, the warmer the spread of the heat of the stones into his arms.

"I cannot immediately determine the value of the stones and give you their value for your mother. I will go home with you and offer you and your mother the two remaining meals for the day while I determine your mum's stone's value. For whatever the gods give any person, the value must take the person through life till she is no more. That is her personal talent. Your children or child will also be given something at the beginning of life, and when you get the right value it takes you through life.

"Your mother is a goddess who wishes to put me through a test to find out whether in my life's walk I will give the right or correct value to everyone I meet. And the eyes only test of value will fail, as they did the first parents, who, when the fruit that was not even theirs, thought that its value was its pleasantness to them. But they did not access the value of what they were been given, whether they will be capable of determining the value and paying for it, but if unable to pay for it, reject it. And to do that they should have gone beyond the eye value assessment and applied the four other sensory assessments as to the fruit's value. But even after that, inquire of a god or goddess as to what value and pay immediately or be tied to paying throughout the giver's lifetime, for none must lack who gives what he has to another."

The boy bowed, took the two meal packages and went home. They ate the first meal and later the second meal. Then the mother asked the son, the teenager, as to whether the man he gave the two stones to spoke and took him home. The teen son answered yes. And the mother said the two stones have bought for her and him, (until he was independent of her and found his own two stones or whatever the god of life decided to give to him to take him through life) meals and everything they will need, for as the man examines the stones with the other senses, he will find more value and therefore the need to pay more or to continue to pay.

The mother and son fell asleep after the second meal. They slept for many months, through the autumn and winter months, and woke up only when spring had started with two days of spring freshness gone.

"And while they slept, Granddad Melon Elembele found that he could by striking the two stones against each other light a flame to cook or warm himself. And he with the two stones went from home to home created flames in homes to warm persons and to cook food, and that begun the first time of humans cooking food and eating cooked food instead raw or uncooked food.

"When he saw the boy at his doorway that spring – I mean Granddad Melon Elembele's doorway – they both stretched their arms and hugged. 'All your meals have been kept for you and your mum,' Granddad said. 'Mum had said that any stored meals be given to others while what is ours is what we would get from today, for the past does not belong to those whose stone's value yields daily, but those who were denied the right assessment of their stone's values,' the teenager said.

"When you didn't visit for many months, each of the two stones I used on the faces of men and women to remove wrinkles, and also acne. They have flawless faces now. And they are also younger looking and have a fresher skin tone. I also used the stones to help those who lack sensitivity to some scents to develop them. And for matters of taste, when the stone was washed into or onto food, the taste of the food was enhanced or tasted better. The two stones each were worth the five senses. And not only that, when the stones were buried in the ground in areas lacking rain, rains fell and watered the grounds sufficiently for bumper harvests for the period. And that's because in a vision of the night, one midnight, I saw a man planting two stones that germinated. I followed that dream because I knew it was a revelation to me not to be missed. I have made many rich. And I have become rich because I received twenty percent of the harvests of their crops. And as I discovered more uses for the two stones, so were their values increased, and so are the rewards for she that offered the stones to me and asked that I determine the values. In that, I know the two stone's values are without limit and can't be paid for.

"And I was able to confirm that the two stones were from a goddess. For gods or goddesses give invaluable things and don't ask for definitive value payment. The wise human, those endowed with wisdom by the gods or goddesses, will not try to short change the gods or goddesses but use what has been handed to them for limitless uses for human benefit."

"Mum said to tell you that you have passed the test for as much as you didn't seek to cheat the gods or goddesses. And so must you not cheat any living thing made in the image of the gods or goddesses or by them," the teenager said, and the mother then entered the Melon Elembele garden and flew in every cardinal direction. And no more were a mother and her teen son seen by Granddad Melon Elembele, but he, Granddad, knew that they saw him every moment.

"At the end of it all, Granddad Melon Elembele spoke saying, 'The gods and goddesses be blessed by whomever that is higher than them or superior to them.'

"And as the inheritors of the Melon brand, we also give and keep giving fruits, houses, hotel rooms and air fares free among many other things, and the people who receive these things also offer us the blessings of the gods and goddesses when they open their mouths to say, 'The gods and goddesses, or they that be higher than the Melon Elembele family, bless them.'

"Melon Jnr, you know that they cannot bless us with their mouths, taking words to the gods and goddesses and turn around to kill or destroy us, as the gods and goddesses don't destroy or kill those they have blessed when after you have received or been sated, asked them to bless."

CHAPTER 13

How to be a son and daughter of the sun

Philadelphia, PA, USA. October 27, 2017

One of the family' s aircraft landed at Tomeni Airport at 10pm local time, so said the pilot. I lowered the shutters to look outside, but saw snow starting to fall. The pilot had not informed us before the flight began as to snowfall at our arrival airport. She didn't mention snow falling either. But we trusted Granddad Melon to solve any emergency or emerging situation.

When Granddad Melon disembarked the aircraft with one of the crew, leaving two hundred select grandchildren by birth or adoption on board for thirty minutes without word, I knew what he would have been doing. He would have taken his socks and shoes off and walked forty feet forwards and returned. Then his knees, both will have touched the ground, the tarmac. And next his forehead will have touched the ground and remained for five minutes. But I wondered what he would do in a snowing place.

When they re-entered the aircraft, I saw particles on his forehead, but his shoes were on his feet. Then I realized the snow could not stop him from what he must do on first arrival in any country.

We disembarked, one by one in a straight line following him, the snow still falling from the purview of our eyes, but not a touch on our heads or any part of our bodies. Did we walk through an enclosed corridor? I didn't see any enclosure.

The host who met us, shook his head when he took Granddad's right hand in his, then let go of Granddad's hand and went on all limbs like an animal – which act, some days later, Granddad said was reserved for the gods or those seen as gods. For the gods acted in particular way when they visited any location, such as what Granddad did on the tarmac. Ah! Granddad was not subject to falling snow. We were not subject to the falling snow. And the cold of snow had no effect on us when we wore not the thick over garments to keep warm.

We ate dinner and retired to our rooms, two sisters per room. No heaters were in our room, Zetumta's and mine. But we felt not cold or hot. It was as if the warmth of the sun and the cold of snow had blended to give us a comfortable temperature of 22.0 degrees Celsius.

Three malls were opened at three different locations over the next four days of our arrival. At each open-air ceremony, the people noted that the elements of nature, such as the sun, wind or cold (snow) had no effect on us, wherever we sat with or without the appropriate clothing. On our last day to depart, a female friend I made asked whether the blood within our bodies changed according to the weather pattern, and therefore we were unaffected adversely by cold or heat. But, not knowing the answer, I answered her that that was an intelligent, deductive question. And so, she expressed the hope that one day scientists could invent a gadget or some drink when put on or drank that could adapt human's blood so that billions are not spent every year during the various seasons to buy seasonal clothing. And in hot weather buying air conditioners to use, or heaters in cold seasons with huge cost implications. I assured her that I would find out what made us different from other humans who were not of the Melon Elembele family stock.

Granddad Melon Elembele incidentally informed me on the flight back home of his having appointed Zewerina (the female who asked the intelligent deductive question) as the country manager for the malls because he found her with unusual intelligence. Because she had questions to ask about the unusual and offered likely answers. He mentioned about her adoption as a

Melon Elembele family member and that it was to be kept in strict confidence.

"That would be great!" I shouted.

"It will be done as you have celebrated. For whatever is proactively celebrated by a granddaughter is a matter revealed by gods or goddesses and only seeking confirmation for it to be done," Granddad said.

"Hmm! Granddad, should it be a secret?" I asked.

"Secrets are surprises. And surprises are gifts that those who are expectant receive, and look for more surprises, and therefore don't rely on only what the five senses can give them," Granddad Melon answered. "And that will be another Melon Elembele family member offering the world the best of everything,"

I smiled at Granddad, who returned to his seat.

Many days after returning to our various homes, I wrote to Granddad simply asking him how to become a son or daughter of the sun, and therefore of snow or water and the wind. He wrote back saying that by submitting to each as a child would to its parents.

And whenever I mentioned the sun by name and said that the sun was my mother, it would give me whatever I asked. At that instant my mind was opened to understand what Granddad Melon Elembele meant. I hope you also understand. Your mind must be opened to grasp what it means, otherwise you can't get or tap the sun for the benefits we had in Tomeni. And so also tap snow or wind for benefits. And that way, our family would not have to make warm clothing to wear to keep warm in cold seasons, or cooler clothing to keep cooler in the hot season times.

It never crossed our minds that you can be a son or daughter of the sun and therefore ask her to accompany you on trips or anywhere you would stay and give you 'clothing' appropriate to maintain an optimum body temperature of 22.0 degree Celsius until that trip with Granddad, and what I learnt through observation and was confirmed through my question.

'And so, a son or daughter...' was one of the hidden insights I, Anna, wrote in my life diary, and mentioned to my husband

Melon Elembele Jnr one of the nights when we had retrospection, before doing other things of night.

CHAPTER 14

The people of the Nation's Church in various countries of the world

Philadelphia, PA, USA. October 28, 2017

A young woman and an elderly man arrived at the people of a nation's church in a location in one country. Nine smiling young women wearing blouses that carried the name Nation's Church (on front and back of the blouse) was as invitingly warm as the warmth of smiles. And if their smiles could be measured on a 'smilometer' it would have recorded the highest reading. And the two visitors hoped in their minds that a good reading in the hearts of the nine women would be the same as on the 'smilometer'. And one by one, the nine smiling young women who happened to be church beverage station attendants and usherettes shook the hands of the two who had entered, and one of them mentioned that there were various beverages and if they could offer any. The elderly man and the young woman answered in the negative.

The man and woman were ushered to chairs at a reception area, because the church auditorium was only opened at a minute to church service opening time, when the priest in charge would be the first to enter, followed by four singers, two women and two men. This was what the two visitors noted when the church service was about to start.

To their surprise and shock, the priest wore no priestly gown but a pair of faded jeans and polo shirt. And he also carried no airs of a priest – though the five young women who stood behind the beverage serving point carried airs of being servers and with a passion, and whether it be of sincerity or not, they and only non-humans could tell.

The four other young women had airs of ushers or usherettes. While seated at the reception area, one usherette asked the young woman with the elderly man as to any other assistance they, frontline staff, the usherettes and beverage stand attendants, could do to make them comfortable.

And so she answered, "I will serve as an usherette, a church entrance usherette." And added, "I will be giving out the church bulletins and welcome cards and shaking members' and visitors' hands alike before entry, according to email sent to me by the Bishop's wife."

"Oh! The bishop's wife does not come to church at this location. I will introduce you to the location pastor's wife and she will receive you and give you orientation," Nita, whose name glistened on her blouse pocket, said.

Nita and the young woman moved to an inner room, leaving the elderly man behind.

"Eh! An usher, with dark coloured skin? She could drive the entering members or visitors away when they see her. They will think it is a witches' coven, or has become one since the previous Sunday church service," one of the beverage stand attendants said.

The rest of the four laughed aloud, then two of them, while dancing, said, "The waltz dance of witches."

A man came to the beverage stand then, and lifted the covers of the beverage containers and put them back on.

"There is a new usherette. Her first time in church. She is dark-coloured," one attendant mentioned to him.

"A dark-coloured usherette?" he asked, as if he didn't hear her correctly. He said no more but he had a frown on his face. But then while moving away from the beverage stand, he said, "I thought ushering was a promotion role. From serving tables, no, beverages, for three years, then you become an usher or usherette."

"The bishop's wife maybe didn't see her skin colour before making this appointment. Is she beautiful or attractive?" the man asked.

"How can someone from the witches' coven be beautiful and attractive? They are always painted as weird-looking and fearful beings. And since I have not seen any in real life, what I have seen and what the artists or painters paint look alike."

"But this one, what we saw, had a charming smile. Hmm! Maybe that is the method they use to enlist members into the church of witchcraft," the same beverage attendant said.

When church service was going on, a large thud was heard from the beverage stand location, followed four other thuds in quick succession, like persons falling on the wooden floor. Then a siren of emergency vehicles was heard, and the ducking of heads of church members between chairs for safety was seen, those within the church hoping that religious non-zealots had not attacked. Then came a loud cry. The paramedics on arrival found the five young women beverage stand attendants dead, persons known to them – the paramedics.

The priest was buzzed and informed. The church service ended abruptly. The congregation fled through the emergency doors when it was realized that it was not the acts of religious non-zealots. The church doors were closed for four weeks as the church authorities and the civil emergency services sought to understand what had happened. The civil emergency services found nothing as to what caused the deaths.

Then the bishop's wife, while in bed on waking up, was reading a scripture at the beginning of the fifth week of the closure of that church-urbane location, when she came across the words: 'For it is time for judgment to begin, starting with the house of God. And if . . .' She didn't read to the verse's end. She got out of bed. "The judgment has begun, as written. This is fulfilment of scripture. Who next?" she cried as the husband rushed towards where her voice was heard.

"We will suspend church services. No, *all* church activities, to be part of the later judgment, not the starting judgment as happened at the urbane location," the bishop said to the wife.

"You've got it wrong. He that saves those who are lost and makes them children also judges and condemns, starting with the House of God. And from the House of God, he would judge those outside it," she said.

"But we in the church of the people of the nations in the various countries of the world are lost because we judge by looking at appearances. Those five must have judged someone wrongly hence their condemnation," the Bishop's wife said.

"You don't know. I have had reports from other branches of strange inexplicable deaths. And that is judgment starting with those in God's house, and not only from our churches, but from a majority of the churches of the people of the nations in the countries of the world. And so far, only branch churches of the family church, and there is only one family church, Melon Elembele, that has not suffered death of some members.

CHAPTER 15

Mawu Sopkolisa's marriage vows with the Melon Elembele family

Philadelphia, PA, USA. October 29, 2017

Throughout the generations, non-members of the Melon Elembele family have not had the opportunity to read, hear or listen to the vows between the family and Mawu Sokpolisa. And when it was for the first time publicized by posting on all Melon Elembele properties across the countries of the world for the people of the nations to read, fear gripped some people of the nations that if they read, or got to know the vows, they would be subject to be judged by them. They reasoned that what you don't know you wouldn't be judged by.

The vows were therefore recorded and played in all properties, both residential, commercial, industrial, and in their aeroplanes, trains, ships, buses, cars – whatever carried the Melon Elembele branded symbol for the benefit of the people of the nations in the various countries of the world. The people of the nations in the various countries of the world then reasoned that marriage vows must be recited between two persons and sealed with an act for it to be a marriage. And they can only be condemned if they recited the marriage vows with Mawu Sokpolisa, the god of the Melon Elembele family and themselves and failed its terms. Then only could they be subject to be punished or disciplined.

The people of the nations' gods in the various countries of the world have subjected them already to many punishments for breaches. And they would not be married to another god by entry into vows with it; they would breach the vows and suffer more. But the more they gave excuses so as not to be judged, the more they felt that the vows had entered into their brains because they kept hearing the words of the vows and also had visions of the vows. Many of them destroyed their eyes and ears, but couldn't destroy their brains, as that would eventually lead to death. They explained the destruction of their two senses as wanting to be like their gods and goddesses that don't hear, see or speak. On doing that, they said they were fools not to have been like their gods many generations earlier, but at a late stage. Then one of their number who advised his family against the destruction of their eyes and ears, but pretended to have destroyed them, used signs to show them over many months that their gods were stones, trees, rocks, things that don't speak or see, hence they couldn't have recited any vows with 'things' and therefore be in a marital relationship for reciprocal benefits.

The god of the Melon Elembele family (Mawu Sokpolisa) hears, speaks, feels, smells and tastes. Hence, they call him the god with five names. Mawu Sokpolisa speaks as the thunder, and they are its words, its taste buds the rays of the sun. It sees with the lightnings, they are its eyes; it smells with the winds, they are its nostrils; and the rains are its sense of touch or feelings. Mawu Sokpolisa's five senses were and are superior to those of humans who live on Earth. But those who married it have that superiority added to their limited five senses and therefore can operate beyond Earth's world. This was an understanding we, the people of the nations in the various countries of the world, didn't realize. We can still seek to know the vows, recite them, and be married to the Melon Elembele god, Mawu Sokpolisa, to have the added benefit of its five superior senses. You agree that marriage makes the married powerful and overcomers, but the unmarried must remain under parental marriage to Mawu Sokpolisa for that added superior protection. And when later they marry as husband and wife to Mawu Sokpolisa, then parental and Mawu Sokpolisa marriage doesn't cover them again.

"Then it is not good to divorce after a husband and wife's marriage to Mawu Sokpolisa," most of them told him.

"But when you divorce, you must renew your vow with Mawu Sokpolisa," I answered, and went for a copy of the vows. "Mawu Sokpolisa, (Almighty God) (Big God); Mawu Sokpolisa (Almighty God), Xebiso (Lightning); Mawu Sokpolisa (Almighty God), Kekleli (There is glory); Mawu Sokpolisa (Almighty God), Gbedidi (The sound); Mawu Sokpolisa, (Almighty God) Tsi (Quench or put out).

"You are the five-names-god. Your fortresses are your names and also weapons for attacks. Your weapons none can withstand, for they are your names. There is no name greater than one of your names, moreover the five names of Mawu Sokpolisa: Olukpe, Ndi (hear in the morning, the rock); Olukpe, Yetroo (hear in the afternoon, the rock); Olukpe, Fie, (hear in the evening, the rock); Olukpe, Za, (hear in the night, the rock); Olukpe, Forforme (hear at dawn, the rock. The vows are recited first at dawn, followed by another recitation at dusk, and Mawu Sokpolisa will concur by thunder or only lightning, or by thunder and lightning. And from that day forward, Mawu Sokpolisa will answer you when you cry out by releasing any of thunder, lightning, sun, wind or water for your protection or defence."

And so, one man of the people of the nations and his relations in various countries of the world, numbering thousands upon thousands, took the vow to follow Mawu Sokpolisa and be like the Melon Elembele family, and later be adopted as members of the Melon Elembele family.

And before their adoption they asked to know Melon Elembele work ethics, and whether it was based on Granddad Melon Elembele ethics or on Mawu Sokpolisa's. And it was explained that it was based on Mawu Sokpolisa's.

CHAPTER 16

The Melon Elembele work ethics are Mawu Sokpolisa's ethics

Philadelphia, PA, USA. October 30, 2017

If every day I will have the mind of Mawu Sokpolisa, I will have the heart of Mawu Sokpolisa, will have the hand of Mawu Sokpolisa and the feet of Mawu Sokpolisa, I will exceed all humans on Earth in my assigned (even of members of my family, the Melon Elembele) portion of work. And Mawu Sokpolisa shall be my god every day. I will praise and dedicate my life to Mawu Sokpolisa in the morning before the start of my work. And in the evening, when I have excellently completed my assigned work, I will thank Mawu Sokpolisa and ask for a sound restful sleep and awesome ideas for the next day's work with Mawu Sokpolisa's help.

And for the many years that the Melon Elembele family came under Granddad Melon Elembele and began to invoke the five-names-god, Mawu Sokpolisa, each day, has been a life of fruitfulness, multiplication and fertility, and expansion of its hold and territory, Melon Elembele Jnr and wife Anna informed us. While I Reklaim, the leader of the people of the nations in the various countries of the world, bowed my head to the ground, and said, "The Earth is filled with your works, and excellence is manifest in all that you do, and your esteem and the glory of Mawu Sokpolisa has been all over the Earth and the heavens."

"But the choice of a god, Mawu Sokpolisa or another, is for all people of the nations in the various countries of the world to make. And the commitment to have the work ethic of a man or woman or of Mawu Sokpolisa and to work like god and as god, Mawu Sokpolisa is also yours, and every person following you to make. And the results you will see and confirm with your other four senses. But all others will see, and not confirm with their four other senses because they are not partaking in your work ethic. It leaves none hungry. It ensures prosperity for all. There is peace all round, non-breakers of laws, and none diseased or sick ever, for hearty laughter and smiles we share every day. And our rest times are celebratory times also. Can you imagine sharing laughter and smiles among all people, every time? Is that not utopia or heaven? We create heaven not by imagination but working and living it," Anna concluded.

"We will go and live like that and as Mawu Sokpolisa in work ethics," their leader said, and left and promised to update us, Melon Elembele family's Anna, Melon Elembele Jnr and Golu Goka on the invoking of Mawu Sokpolisa and the work ethics.

"Twelve months went by without a word from them. But we knew that if they did the work as unto Mawu Sokpolisa, the farmers, fishermen and women and other agricultural workers would have noticed multiple harvests. Enjoying better sleep. Better relationships. Everything exceeding their expectations. Because where it was Mawu Sokpolisa, the unusual became the norm. The thoughts of our minds didn't end when we heard the laughter of men, women and children and saw their smiles on the Melon vision monitor. They were at a celebration festival celebrating one year of awesome goodness, because that one year gave them more than twenty years combined when they were part of the people of the nations and served the nations gods and goddesses, but were disappointed and dissatisfied with their jobs, the jobs added sorrow and gave not enough because they worked to human employers. And when we heard the chief celebrant's concluding remarks, we were stunned that we left yearly celebration out, as it was the leader's wife who spoke the words: 'At work we were satisfied and looked forward to next many days or nights work. At rest, it was so refreshing that after only two hours rest, some wanted to go back to work, but in reverence to Mawu Sokpolisa, everyone took the full-time rest and the associated Mawu Sokpolisa benefits.'

"We were joyous that we had led some of the people of the nations to Mawu Sokpolisa, and Mawu Sopkolisa had done what has been done over the years to us to them also, what Mawu Sokpolisa's work ethic does," Anna concluded.

CHAPTER 17

Granddad's five tests involving some family members

Philadelphia, PA, USA. October 31, 2017

F|ive years into the usage of portable technology devices by all members of the Melon Elembele family, he invited one female granddaughter and one male grandson from each country of the two hundred countries the Melon Elembele various companies operate in, members of his family, for a weekend retreat of knowing how their brains were functioning. As each arrived in his home, he called each by name, mentioned both parent's names, and the city and country of their residence without a look at a gadget. And with all arrived, they slept overnight without any distraction, except the dinner each requested in advance which was prepared.

At breakfast, for all four hundred, he announced that it would be a five-course meal and that there would be five tests of each. And only those who pass the five tests will eat breakfast with him. They all clapped. And he then asked as to those who had brought their all-knowing technology tablets to breakfast. All hands were raised.

"Oh! The world has come far. Technology intrudes and distracts even at breakfast?" he asked.

"Granddad, not only at breakfast but at all meal times. Even our parents come with it to meals," some grandchildren said.

"Am I that elderly as to not know what is happening during the time of the gadgets?" Granddad asked.

"Granddad, age is not showing on you in senility, grey hairs, loss of memory of things of the past, because you remembered our faces and called us by name and more than that. And the things of the future will also be within your grasp if Alzheimer's, the disease of the elderly, excludes you from its effects," a granddaughter called Merian said.

"Oh no, Alzheimer's is not a disease for the elderly and of the elderly. It is what you do with your mind. Because, for example, when you exercise your body parts – I play golf and I swim – your body parts remain physically fit and easy to move. But I know that some have fallen and died when, without regular exercise of physical nature, they tried to carry heavy objects or wrestled with an attacker. Well, let us take the tests. It is a test of honour. You will all answer the same five questions, each question consisting of ten other questions."

And he took a bag, took each technology tablet from each of them, and put it in it. And it was carried away to another room.

"I am not to call names from A to Z, neither from Z to A. It will be randomly done. Geeta, your five questions and the ten questions under it are: family life. What is your Granddad's full name, your parent's full names, and their cell numbers. And what are the cell numbers of nine other members of Melon Elembele?" he asked.

"Please skip. I will not eat breakfast. I would rather fast. I will not even listen to the next four questions consisting of ten other questions. The answers to your questions could be found on my cell phone just by tapping. Granddad, you didn't warn us not to store everything on cell tablets but some in our personal memory. You and our parents have not been fair to us. You should rather have given them the test," Geeta said.

"I will proceed to question two for the benefit of the rest. Question two is on our industries: What is the most visibly seen industry carrying the Melon brand? And can you name ten countries, in alphabetical order, that we operate in?" Granddad asked.

Theguna raised both hands and suggested that Granddad should ask the remaining three major questions so that they could all answer it on paper in the old-fashioned way. He, without consulting the other grandchildren, expressed further that it may be a day of fasting for all them, not only of breakfast but of other meals too, and a fast of not using technology tablets so as to get to know each other's name and try to store it in their human mind or brain.

"You have spoken for all of us," Ranbow said, and asked whether the technology manufacturers should not provide a warning notice on their devices that your natural brain keeps no memory of events, names, places etc., and will fail you when your technology device is taken away from you.

But Granddad said, "And my third question is on languages and cultures. What is the language spoken by most members of Melon Elembele family? List the nine other languages spoken by the Melon Elembele family.

"Question four will seek for your understanding of the two races. And list the nine different geographic zones occupied by the two races.

"And my final question, question five, is on the social life of people. And list nine factors that enhance social cohesion of people."

Geeta had gone to Granddad's office and taken one ream of four hundred sheets and distributed it to each of them.

After a ten-minute wait by Granddad, no sheet was handed in by any. He therefore retrieved the bag the tablets were kept in, and as he took them out, one by one, he mentioned its owner's name without looking at any identifying mark, and finished all four hundred names from his memory.

And with a self-imposed fast that morning, each left his or tablet and spent the rest of the day going through the garden chatting and asking questions about trees, flowers, insects and flies and birds, so as to be like Granddad who would not enslave his brain to a gadget, because whatever takes your memory away, leaves you with no knowledge for a future war that it will win, without any shot.

And so it was that after that fast day, four hundred grandchildren administered tests to others, and billions, on failing, went back to practise a time for everything on Earth so as not to be subject to any but be above all.

CHAPTER 18

Time and tide; every Melon Elembele knows; we were not taught

Philadelphia, PA, USA. November 1, 2017

When I sat under those trees clustered as if in love with them, I remembered the love for Anna and her love for me. But as the tree grows without any of us seeing the tree growth, so I knew that love must grow without being seen to be growing. I noticed that the tree had the sunlight on it every day, without protesting or raising concern. And so also did I realize that the wind and the rain also come at it, that it knew that from its birth it must live in harmony with different elements to survive. Could the tree make a selection of things it needs and things it doesn't need? The tree puts its roots in the ground because it knows it must receive from the ground as it must receive above the air also. Then I saw a bird, an eagle fly into the tree, without making a home in that tree, because it was not the season to make a home. For it requires a home for only its eggs and hatchlings, and for a season and then move on elsewhere leaving its young, but whom must find their own home.

With my knowledge of the trees and of the eagle, I went to the seashore to learn from it. I stood on its clean sandy beaches, enthralled by the quiet waves and their boundaries, not knowing who kept it in check. I saw no rough waves for hours. I was ready to return home and tell everyone I met that the sea is of calm disposition. But the next few minutes made me change my mind. There arose a tide, then another, and I realized then that tide waits not for anyone. It pleases no one with its beauty; whether it is praised or not it comes at its time, and will come again and again. And I also learnt that even with the tides or waves, it goes not beyond its tide boundaries or wave boundaries. And again, the tide also taught me that it plays within timelines.

On my return home from the beach, I wondered how someone who lives not near the sea, would know about the tides and apply its lessons to learn life's lessons. Then walks in, she who has lived only in the forest. I asked her as to when the forest is greenest, or when its leaves turn brown. She, without answering my question, looked mournfully at me. I mentioned to her about the tides and times. She, in turn, spoke about the times various insects come out in the night but not when the sun's rays rise majestically.

"Oh," I said, "there is a tide in everything. You must wait for it. It will not wait for you. The low tide must be keep within its boundary, and the high tide within its boundary. Then I asked she who had come from the forest as to whether she lived alone. She answered saying she was married with children, and that when you see beauty in the low tide, so must you see beauty in the high tides, so that your moods will not fluctuate: one time a happy person, another time a depressive. She described the different scenes of the tides, and urged me to be expectant of the tides and react appropriately to any. She who lived in the forest but not ever near the sea, explained that when you see the high tide coming at you, there is fear that it will swallow you and carry you in its 'belly' away to drown you, so you therefore flee some distance away and then return. But you don't flee at the low tide. She said to study the tides and apply their lessons to marriage between humans. Know when to move a bit away, or to speak in a particular way so as not to anger the tide.

The trees have lived with the tides of the sun and also of the wind and rain, without anyone walking out on the other, when, without the symbiotic relationship, all would be at risk of not living long on Earth. Then I remembered that Granddad had spoken about the different types of tides. But to seek help on the high tide as much as you will a low tide, and if you lack understanding of tides in human relationships, I was glad in my spirit and body that the Melon Elembele family have been successful at everything because of the foundation Granddad Melon laid, whether it be low or high tide in any type of human relationship.

When Anna returned from a visit to some family members and I told her of the reasoning or thinking exercise I did, she explained that that was why Granddad Melon avoided artificial gadgets or tablets which offer applications to enslave you, making you not independent of its features but totally dependent, making you lose all memory and develop a violent disposition because you no longer know your relations as relations. For what you attach value to in your mind and are obsessed with, you preserve and protect.

"Time and tide every Melon Elembele knows," she said, as if she was around when the husband had made a similar statement.

It then dawned on me, upon further reflection, that I was all the time alone: no woman had come from the forest to speak with me. It was my mind that carried out those various thought processes, to keep it sharp, unlike the dependence on tablets and cells, when it reasons not or exercises not again.

"I will keep the various tides in memory and in view so as not to lose in the world of technology, where it is easy to avoid some tides," I then self-spoke.

CHAPTER 19

Granddad Melon Elembele's first envelope of words for the future unsealed

Philadelphia, PA, USA. November 2, 2017

When Anna unlocked the safe that mid-morning and said, "Women are entrusted with precious documents and pearls, (and some are worth more than pearls), to keep safe till a season when they would be required." And she safely and intact produced the documents, waved them around for physical eyes of humans and seeing eyes of other things of nature, such as trees, birds, flies, and cockroaches among others, to confirm that they had seen that she had faithfully kept what was entrusted to her.

But the opening of the envelope, or its unsealing and the reading of the contents, are for the husband or a male relative, so that she being detail-oriented hears. And as she says the 'Ahs' and the 'Ohs' at what she is hearing, she also faithfully stores it in heart and memory for later recollection and sharing to others through conversation, just in case a strange fire – a fire the source of which is not known, or a fire that does not come from natural sources to trigger it – burns the document to destroy the insight that was to be made available for further human enlightenment and progress.

"And I can, by a woman's intuition, tell you, my husband, that Granddad Melon Elembele's words in the unsealed envelope will transport us to the final enlightenment period and progress where there will be no physical impediment in humans' ability," she added.

"Anna, since I don't know what is in it, let me take . . ." He broke off the sentence, hugged her for minutes, and said, "Hugs are a buffer against the unknown."

"Gee, I thought you were going to take another step and go all out and drink the fountain of youthfulness and youth," Anna said.

"Oh! Not all. After the unsealing, new methods may be revealed for doing it and we will be transported in the joined state to another part of the universe where they are permanently in that state," Melon Jnr answered.

"That will be heavenly. We could ask Mawu Sokpolisa to create that type of heaven where they marry and not the one where they don't marry or are not given in marriage," Anna enthusiastically expressed.

"Eh, this is just conjecture. I think in heaven that they don't marry or are given in marriage because those who have failed to enjoy marriage on Earth should not be allowed to continue the failure in heaven, a place of bliss. But those who have won a crown on Earth in marriage can put in a plea like we did when the sexes didn't have equal numbers on Earth to be in marriage there also, the permanently joined state," Melon Jnr suggestively said.

"The envelope is still in your hand, unsealed or unopened. Open it for its treasures, to ensure the benefit of the Melon Elembele family," Anna told the husband.

"I am using a pair of scissors to cut all four sides. Four is the number of perfection. And what will come out of the envelope will make us perfect in some way—"

"Wow, a husband prophet? Or only an expression of hope?" Anna interjected to ask.

"Whatever holy men, or sacred men, no, holy humans said in the past, Mawu Sopkolisa permitted to pass and changed the destinies of nations from bad state to a good state," Melon Jnr stated.

"Then let whatever we both say, be," Anna responded.

One sheet of writing dropped to the floor and Melon Jnr bent over to pick it. And Anna expressed her sadness that the husband dropped the writing to the floor, stating that if he had sought her opinion as to how to hold the envelope, whether horizontally or vertically before cutting it open, she would have advised the horizontal mode.

"Oh, the material with writing on is a cloth like material to the touch. I don't know what cloth material it is," Melon Jnr said.

"The answer to your lack of that knowledge lies with a woman, I, your wife. But the contents first must be read aloud. And then you pass the material to me to tell you what its name is and what it is made of," Anna advised.

"I will read–" Melon Jnr was saying, when Anna interjected to say, "That sounds too formal in a husband and wife setting. Start again, but in a way that can make me fall again in love with you, a renewal or fresh love. You can make a woman or wife renew her love, or give you fresh love, every day by your acts or words. But don't do anything that will make you fall asleep while reading," Anna admonished.

"Anna, Granddad's first unsealed envelope is opened, and has revealed it all: 'Dear children and grandchildren, what humanity seeks is to be like Mawu Sokpolisa. But humans don't know the way to be as Mawu Sokpolisa. We have as a family made strides to that end. But others have not. Because they make technological gadgets, thinking that the more advanced those gadgets, the more likely it will be that they will be like Mawu Sokpolisa, and be Mawu Sopkolisa. But those things they make are material things – things that can be touched, handled or felt. And things that can be destroyed by the sun's rays, be destroyed by wind or water or thunder and also by lightning, cannot put you in the same status as Mawu Sokpolisa. What you need to do is to "harness" – a word from Mawu Sokpolisa – when you have achieved a certain level, the level where your words are sacred and when you speak, Mawu Sopkolisa, voids not it. Then Mawu Sokpolisa gives you that one expression: Ra-ra-ra. And when spoken you are transported in a different body, the body of Mawu Sokpolisa across the heavens, waters, on land, and the various planets, but not in any human mode of transportation. And finally, you make your dwelling closer to the sun, un-burnt, because of your new body, the Mawu Sokpolisa body. Measure your words when Mawu Sokpolisa voids them not, then you can use the words, Ra-ra-ra, and the incidents earlier stated will happen, and you will make your dwelling next to the sun.'

"What will I render to a woman who listens attentively and takes every word into her heart and mind, I will render . . ."

Without completing the sentence, he planted kisses all over her body, and handed over the cloth-like material to her for her answer.

But then she said, "Not now. I am tired. Another time. The opportune time. And I will disclose it to you."

CHAPTER 20

The present is a gender; the future is a gender

Philadelphia, PA, USA. November 3, 2017

The Havina people were all males. Five thousand of them. We knew not that humans who look no different from us lived in a cleared area in a mangrove forest. When Granddad's aircraft flew over the mangrove on our monthly recreational flight, the pilot mentioned that he had sighted two tall men walking naked and that Granddad's desire to acquire the area for a zoo may not materialize.

Granddad ordered the pilot to release the 'Loni' powder over a stretch of one thousand feet by three hundred feet on the stream from its belly on a stream seen not far from the mangrove and land the aircraft. (Because when the Loni powder is spread in a rectangular form, it spreads from one end to the other and hardens into a pad hard enough to land their 747-800 aircraft on.) The pilot from the left side of the aircraft released the Loni powder as suggested, and within ten minutes, a landing pad was in place and we landed.

"Your Granddad Melon lived ahead of his times, and later my Granddad. His memory won't ever be erased. He did wonderful things. Release a powder that hardens to form a tarmac to land an aircraft on? No doubt the Melon brand keeps expanding through new inventions. To your knowledge, did the people of the nations in the various countries of the world also have such ability to create a tarmac to land on within minutes?" Melon Jnr asked.

"Please, don't rush me. Be patient, for the patient will have everything that they must have. But the impatient makes you skip

71

some facts and denies himself or herself complete or full knowledge. And when placed in a similar situation, has no know-how or requisite knowledge to deploy to solve a challenge. We landed on the stream tarmac—"

"Oh! Anna, one question before you continue," Melon Jnr interrupted her to say.

"And what is your question?" Anna asked.

"Could the tarmac thus created be removed and the stream does not then have an island within it?" Melon Jnr asked.

"Whatever Granddad Melon does, he is capable of undoing. He does not destroy what nature has endowed the world. Think of what he instructed the pilot to do to undo the tarmac. You are a Melon. But no more interruptions.

"We walked to the banks of the stream. Granddad washed his face with the water from the stream. I also did. And the pilot copied us. Then a ray of the sun shown at a forty-five-degree angle cast a shadow on the ground," Anna mentioned.

"This is the way to go. Mawu Sokpolisa has created a path for us. The path will lead us to what we must see," Granddad said, and led the way, but after two minutes asked that I be beside him. I did. Seven miles on, we both noticed two men squatting in the mangrove. They saw us. They made a guttural noise, and there was loud whistling around us, which made the birds fly from their resting places with so many squawks, and moved onto the stream.

"Then the two men stepped out, moving very fast. We moved after them. They stood in a cleared area from the distance that we were at and we saw others joining them. They were many. And when we got closer to a hearing distance from them, Granddad spoke a language I had not heard him speak before to any of us. They must have understood him, because they all sat on the ground, and said certain words that Granddad later explained were numbers that each of them was known by. And they had sat down in reverence to him because they felt I, Anna, and he were gods who had come to their habitation.

"Granddad didn't tell them that I am no god. But later told me that he did that because a person may not be a god in his family, or today, but would be revered as a god by some others or some time. Granddad said some other things, and after twenty more minutes, they stood up and followed us back to the aircraft, but at distance that they could see the aircraft. They began to crawl on the their limbs. And once aboard the aircraft, but not Granddad then, the pilot taxied and we were airborne, but stationary at three thousand feet. Granddad took his two stones and hit them on a spot on the tarmac and, gradually, it turned back into powder and followed a vertical track or path back into its hold for use another time. Fifteen minutes later, Granddad joined us in the aircraft. Don't ask me how. I don't know. Maybe he tamed gravity."

"Did he create the zoo on that land?" Melon Jnr asked.

"We did. All the people died one after the other within a space of three years. And Granddad 's explanation was that no disease killed them, neither did he kill them. He said the people – all of them males – died because males are called the 'present'. But women were and are called the 'future' in the books of Mawu Sokpolisa. And any present without a future has no prospect of regenerating and will die. Men are the present, because they don't give birth and therefore life. But women are the future, because they give birth and life. And so, there are two genders, and one is the future," Granddad concluded.

"I am a gender. I am the future," Anna said.

"What an insight! Then I can't do away with you," Melon Jnr said.

"A world without women is a world without a future and no men," Anna explained.

CHAPTER 21

The seven-star women of Vicrata

Philadelphia, PA, USA. November 4, 2017

They fell backwards and on their backs (supine), exposing their underwear to the sight of the men who gathered with the loud roars of our aircraft landing. The unkind wind, or possibly they themselves, ripped their stunning blouses of different colours showing different sizes of spellbinding, attractive breasts as they laid on the ground motionless, but not dead, because their skin tones didn't begin to look blue.

I held Granddad' s right hand in my right hand, facing him, and asked what the matter was with the stunning, beautiful women who had fallen on their backs, but not only that, but had exposed their breasts. I didn't receive an answer to my question. It appeared Granddad was thinking about what answer to give. He had a distant look on his face. And within two minutes we heard the sirens of what would be many sixty-seater coaches arrive. Two men from each coach put a manacle on the hands of as many women as they were able to manacle both hands behind their backs and helped them after to stand up (their breasts outside the blouses), and boarded the coaches. When the coaches drove away, Granddad broke his silence.

"They have been arrested for indecent exposure of their breasts to seeing eyes of men, because the breasts of a seven-star woman of Vicrata must not be seen in public under any circumstances," Granddad said.

"Why?" I asked.

"It was not their fault that they fell on their backs and exposed their underwear and therefore breasts. Something, maybe the wind or some object pushed against them?" Anna asked.

"You are yet young, and do not understand everything that is explained to you. I will not offer you an explanation in detail now, but just to say that when the gods intend to punish you for rejecting some of your five senses, they can make you first to fall foul of the law of humanity and take you out of society, jail you or banish you. And if you don't mend your ways, then take away the other senses also. . ."

Granddad paused in his explanation. And I saw the thousands of men file away in threes in silence as if part of their life had been taken away and silence would restore it. But with them, in the distance, Granddad explained their silence as an imposition by the gods that when you see your enemy losing ground, or under possible destruction, keep silence, utter silence, so that the gods will not abandon what they are about to do or started doing.

And being left to ourselves, Granddad asked that we move to his house some two miles away from the landing area.

Once home, we showered, changed our clothes, ate, and he resumed giving reasons for what befell the women.

"Without the senses, men and women and other living things are but like a piece of chalk or other writing instrument in the hands of a teacher. It feels nothing. It hears not anything, and does not see when it is becoming shorter with usage to complain that it will be killed or maimed. I will take you to the city of Vicrata many years ago prior to today.

"The women of Vicrata were adored and praised by their men. Some men hugged them when they saw them in the alleyways, or in churches, and praised their creator for such beauties. Even neighbouring nations' men travelled to Vicrata only to take a look at them and praise them for their stunning bodies. Afraid that they were not comparable to these women, none dared to touch them with a finger, moreover hug them or think of kissing them, and returned to their countries.

"It was the visitors from the four neighbouring nations that called them the 'seven-star women' of Vicrata.

"When I went to open the Melon brand of diverse industries in the country of Zamba, I heard of these wonderful women. Vicrata was not a location for any Melon-branded industry. But I decided to pay a visit to see these awesome or stunning women. And I agreed that the seven-star rating given to them was right. In my eyes, your grandmother could not even earn one star if she stood against any woman of Vicrata. But I am man whose knowledge of Mawu Sokpolisa makes me abhor pride based on image or looks, for as much as you didn't fashion yourself. It is the potter who must show pride, but not the pot. I knew pride would enter them and destroy them with time. And so, when I heard some years later that the rules had changed in Vicrata and men could not praise such beautiful, no, stunning women, or hug them or kiss them at the women's invitation or request, I wept for them, the stunning women of Vicrata.

"Many men were jailed or paid heavy sums for complimentary words spoken years earlier to the hearing of these women. Even men with whom they voluntarily had sex previously, twenty years earlier, when the law was later changed, were executed for taking advantage of them, (the seven-star women), contrary to their seven-star-women's refusal of sexual intercourse.

"The men cried with their hands clasped over their heads for thirty nights and asked that a law, with limited application, be passed to partially protect them. And that is the law that led to their, the seven-star-women's, arrest.

"Anna, I am not done with you. The creator who made them, knowing that the women didn't like two of the human senses given to them, first made them deaf so they would not hear. Anna, again, you know that sweet words make you look prettier. For the words keep adding value to you. It is like being blessed by the words of the people of the nations in the various countries of the world as against no words of admiration from a village of people. You will with time look stunning, because like a flower that is watered to look more beautiful, you have been watered with words to look stunning.

"Next to go was their sense of feel or touch. And when that happened, the insects that lived in the homes of kings and queens at the dry season, not only stung them but gave them blisters, followed by sores and such smells that they nearly asked for the sense of smell to be taken from them.

"They died leaving behind a few thousands. And those were the women I asked Mawu Sokpolisa to give another opportunity to, for a few years, so that the men could find them admirable, marry them, and save the race of these rare women of Vicrata from extinction. But when they saw their 'glory' restored, they forgot that the law on exposure had not been repealed, and condemned the men in their hearts at the time when we had landed and disembarked from the aircraft.

"I don't know what will happen to them in prison as regards their restored sense of hearing and sense of feel (touch). The gods could take them away again."

"Thanks, Mawu Sokpolisa, there are no such women in the Melon Elembele family," Anna said.

"I would not have permitted it. I would have taught them about the usefulness of the five senses and that they were made for our human good," Granddad said.

"Anna, that story kept me mute for, how many hours? Four hours. Good to have a Granddad who knows," Melon Jnr said, then got up and said, "You are a seven-star woman and wife, but different."

CHAPTER 22

Taming or grooming

Philadelphia, PA, USA. November 5, 2017

"Granddad has taught us (especially me) so much that were I to decide to write a book, it would be so voluminous that it would fill his vessel M.V. Manka, the largest seagoing vessel of twelve football fields by four football fields, and therefore three times the size of the largest naval carrier of that nation that straddles as many time zones, as to be second to the Melon Elembele family that straddles all time zones," Anna was heard saying when the husband entered her study.

"Are you conversing with one of your sisters and therefore one of my sisters?" Melon Jnr asked.

"It was self-speak. And you entered at right time. If you don't mind, I could share with you what Granddad Melon Elembele did with regard to many of the granddaughters."

Anna didn't wait for his response, but went on to say, "Granddad had a thousand eagles on his farm in every country of the world in which the Melon Elembele family had operations of one sort or the other."

"An eagle farm?" Melon Jnr asked surprise.

"He tried his hand at every conceivable and inconceivable thing. Some, so as to teach words of wisdom to the unwise. With the eagle farms, he entrusted each farm to a thousand sisters to tame or groom the eagles – meaning one eagle to a sister. You do understand that was each a granddaughter? Happily, I had no eagle under my care. I don't know why he did that. Maybe he knew I would appreciate a theoretical lesson taught and accept it.

"The eagles, as if they had met and agreed, flew away from every farm in all countries at the same time one day. It meant nobody was able to tame or groom her assigned eagle. Granddad was angry at losing his precious eagles, and scolded the granddaughters and asked that they should each go and look for her assigned eagle, as when he (Granddad) was looking after each farm, or through male agents, no eagle was lost or flew away. And that meant that he either had tamed them to become pets who would no more act like eagles and fly away to a habitation high above the clouds in the sky, or, alternatively, he had groomed them to be like humans and therefore not have any thought that the sky is their habitation. He explained that taming was important. And so also grooming. You groom another to be like you and live like you. But you tame another not to be like you, but to behave differently from its environment.

"He then asked all of them as to who wished to be like Granddad, and also achieve the greatness of Granddad, if not greater than Granddad. They all yelled, 'yes', 'yes', and 'yes'.

"Well, the eagles are gone because they saw other eagles in the sky and from the sky they groomed the eagles on the farms to be like them and live like them. I, Granddad Melon Elembele, truly kept them on the farms with an invisible canopy that prevented them from seeing other eagles and so be groomed as eagles and live the life of eagles. But when I handed over the farms to you, granddaughters, I removed the invisible canopies, and that made them able to see, hear and take grooming lessons from the eagles in the sky. And that was the loss of the eagles."

"Eh, grooming is so important. Grooming puts you at your right place!" the girls or sisters shouted. "Then was established a grooming regime in the family. Granddad had timelines for everything. He had times to wear white or other coloured clothing, times when to do what and how fast. We girls spent hours doing our hair. Longer still, to make a choice of what to wear, what shoes, what bags or what sizes. Many such like. There were irritations with ourselves at times, which led to anger and therefore outbursts at other sisters. We all could tell what Granddad wore on each day of the week. How fast or slow certain things work. You know what? He did the cooking and washing at times. And so there went an undisclosed regime of grooming. We copied him, we listened to him, and within two years, we asked for family uniforms, working types and out-of-work types. We took the same time as sisters or granddaughters to do what brothers or grandsons did or will do.

"And whereas we erroneously thought that as sisters or granddaughters we should be unlike our brothers, our grooming taught us that in the nature of only sexual expression, that sisters or granddaughters were and are different from grandsons or brothers in the Melon Elembele family—"

Anna was interrupted by the husband interjecting to say, 'Oh! That is why I lagged behind you most times. But when I began to copy your indirect and unmentioned grooming, I am no more irritated."

"The world of a Granddad is also the world of granddaughters and grandsons through grooming," Melon Jnr said.

CHAPTER 23

Exposure yet disciplined

Philadelphia, PA, USA. November 7, 2017

"Granddad had been married for ten months when he had to go on a long trip of many months. He didn't have any memory of sexual health celebration or sharing to carry with him and therefore will have gone in the strength of that for the many months.

"Grandma didn't like to be touched or hugged. It was as if she was made a nun from birth from the wedding night, when out of excitement of being in a new state of marriage she showered and walked from the bath in her 'splendour' and she kissed him and other things happened and her virginity was broken by him. But she cried the rest of the night till the sun shone, and she stepped out and smiled at the sun, possibly afraid that if she didn't do that the sun in anger could deny her warmth, though she denied her husband the warmth of sexual health celebration. And, for the next nine months, she offered herself once, but at the time, staring at the distant moon and stars as if they were in the bedroom to be admired.

"Melon Jnr, when the gods wish to tempt you and Mawu Sokpolisa wishes to redeem you with power, the gods offer you the best and the exceptional, and that was why, so far, only one human being has been able to overcome the temptation of sexual health celebration by a woman, but all others of wealth, position and ruling kingdoms and nations. Would he have overcome the temptation if it was woman, dark-skinned, light-skinned or coloured with the 'drapings' on her chest and more elsewhere, a person who was made and placed next to him? I will not think of what he would have done or not done. I have so far not read of any man or heard of any man who succeeded when bone of his bones (a woman in her 'birthday' splendour and glory) was placed next to him, except the one whose story you will hear to the end.

"And so, Granddad arrived in Lycia. He was to lodge with a woman called Janus in her apartment. She met him at the dock when his ship berthed. I don't know why a man was to lodge with a woman? Maybe there were no men, or, if there were, they were not the hospitable type. And as for private paid lodgings, there were none those years. She drove him home. And her warmth was unsurpassed at dinner and during conversations pre-bedtime. She allowed him to shower before her. And when she did, she came out from the shower wearing nothing. She asked him to follow her to the bedroom. There was only one. And the walk to the bedroom, him following with eyes unable to turn in any other direction but on her, lifted his spirit out of this world. She sat on the bed and pointed him to sit on a chair directly opposite her.

"She took a vase of coconut oil and began to dab her body with it, while intermittently rubbing it in, and it made her sparkle, giving inviting rays of romance. When she was finished with her arms and legs and began 'work" on her breasts, beautifying them, she would dab and rub in and palpate and then shake. Granddad didn't know that the showering and beautifying by her took two long hours, enough for impatience to arise, yielding anger and a quarrel with a wife (if it were a wife) for wasting time. But he didn't notice it. He actually thought she had taken fifteen minutes and expressed how fast she had been. She laid on the bed. And he had to lie by her. And as he did, their bodies touched. He had wished Mawu Sokpolisa had not created the sense of feel to feel the touch of her body. At that instant, he also wished that if he had a spell, or the power to suspend the sense of feel, he would have suspended it. And other senses that could create challenges needing solution. He remembered he carried no memories of sexual health celebration to neutralize what he was seeing and feeling, or at least reduce their intensity.

"As she chatted with him, she used her body parts a lot to emphasize some points, and therefore he was experiencing more body touches that night than in ten months of freshly being married. She, however, made no attempt to roll over and be on top of him, or forced to go under him or any posture suitable. They fell asleep. He was the first to wake up. But not a hostess, he closed his eyes in pretended sleep and snoring. Thirty or so minutes later, she roused from sleep and walked to the bathroom without a nightie (not that she wore a nightie during the night) or a morning gown. She did all that a woman would do in the morning as first things. She then went back to the room, tapped him, and on opening his eyes, she asked him to do morning hygiene so that they could have breakfast. She prepared the breakfast unclothed while he stood near her in the kitchen. She put on a morning gown when the breakfast table was laid. And they ate, with her asking him whether he had a restful night, to which he answered yes.

"In Granddad's mind's eye, sleep, deep sleep, is the only antidote to not using force or cunningness on a woman such as Janus to have sexual health celebration with her without her expressed words, or acts, or she either kissing you on the lips for two minutes or more, or hugging you tight with breathlessness rising in her, as that would be an indication that you could have more with her, and other body parts, but alert to any, no, no from her, otherwise you would be charged with rape. Because looking at and admiring the body of an accessible, beautiful naked woman was not a contract for sexual health celebration, or sharing, but an invitation to only look and admire.

"Granddad knew his bounds. And when he later heard that all the six billion men on Earth who dreamt about Janus wanted to have sexual health celebration with her, if even only once, he expressed the hope that all men would know the boundary markers between looking and admiring, and looking and admiring and doing.

"A month passed. Janus took rightfully her liberties. For she was in her own home and on her own bed. She, at times, was in the shower with him or he stood in the shower room while she showered with them chatting.

"The three months with Janus came to an end and Granddad returned home. Janus was no more seen on Earth after Granddad's three-month stay with her. Her apartment is a museum that Granddad created in her honour, not her memory, because Janus didn't die but lives in another universe.

"This is the lesson Granddad taught. Exposure, yet discipline every man must face, to be in the will of Mawu Sokpolisa and then be granted lookalike Januses if Mawu Sokpolisa desires.

"And now, my husband, how many days will you spend with Janus and not be Granddad or be a Granddad?" Anna asked.

"Have you asked your other brothers or other grandsons that question? Granddad went through the temptation for me. Also, Janus does not live on Earth again for that exposure and yet discipline," Melon Jnr answered.

And Anna then answered as follows, "They have all heard the story from Granddad or from me. Men, exposure, yet discipline is required, if shadow Januses should visit Earth again, or are living on Earth. Remember, she always has the final say. If at any time during the sexual health celebration, or sharing, she uses words, saying 'stop, stop' you must, though your hope be dashed or be deferred. Pray she uses not words ever," Anna advised.

CHAPTER 24

Mawu Sokpolisa and unexplained events

Philadelphia, PA, USA. November 6, 2017

"Melon Jnr, I will speak about Granddad one more time and until you ask me to continue to honour his memory, or to remind you of his memory by speaking on events I witnessed or he told me, I will not speak about those I have not spoken about to you," Anna said.

"Who in the Melon Elembele family will not want to listen to all about Granddad? I am not prepared to lose my sense of hearing, become deaf and a while later, if I should decide not to speak to others with my mouth, err against Mawu Sokpolisa, and therefore lose the sense of speaking (speech) also. Anna, what pleases you, pleases me, and it radiates to all members of the family. Whatever I was not present with him to witness, I will hear spoken about. And whatever I was present to hear with my ears, I will gladly hear again to enrich me with wisdom and knowledge," Melon Jnr responded.

"I will speak today, skip some days, and come back to speak on things about Granddad that members of other families should listen to if they are to redeem their families, or if they wish to become Melon Elembele adoptees.

"Granddad Melon had started operations in 193 countries, but the beginning of some were eerie, some fearful, some adventurous, and some dramatic, depending on who witnessed them or heard them. In one country he visited, Zewna, when he went to look at a parcel of land near a river independently of anyone – he did that so he could be spoken to by Mawu Sokpolisa to confirm what he was about to do, or for Mawu Sokpolisa to give a sign of approval – he saw an elliptical clay basin having a volume for fifty gallons of water, five feet above the ground, and not held or supported by any anchor or pillar.

"The rain from the clouds was not falling and there was no water tap fixed and opened above the elliptical clay bowl for water to fill the bowl, but the bowl was filling, and a hand with a calabash was scooping the water into an unseen container. He was transfixed to the spot from about 7:00 am till 5:00 pm, when he bowed his head slightly to the ground and felt a release of his feet. He moved to ten inches of the elliptical bowl, cupped both hands, and took water and drank to quench his thirst; then, with both hands again cupped, he fetched water and washed his face. He went on his knees, bowing his head and touching the ground with his forehead five times. His face, unwashed of the sand particles that had stuck to it, he retraced his footsteps back to his lodging not ever turning to look backwards at what he had witnessed.

"That was thirty years before my birth to him. He knew that if the gods must speak to you, you must not eat or do anything associated with the ground and incidents related to ground, so therefore he ate not, or slept not, to possibly see and hear what the god (Mawu Sokpolisa) would convey to him in his car or bedroom.

"Three hours later, in a vision, he saw images of workmen and women putting up a building, the foundations of which he could determine with his physical eyes. He thanked Mawu Sokpolisa for the insight. At dawn, he ate and returned home. Many varied buildings covering three-miles-square were constructed on that land with parking slots. We have also added to it land space and more buildings," Anna said and paused.

"I cannot speak words, neither can I mutter but keep a golden silence for some minutes, taking in what has been said and allow my imagination to add to it. That is meditation," Melon Jnr said.

Fifteen minutes went by before Anna's lips opened again.

"Granddad wanted to build hotels and apartments, a sea port, an inland port, and the biggest airport in Nabunda as it has a beautiful coastline and three rivers criss-crossing the land, but had a population of only fourteen women.

"Granddad wanted to visit the location where the women had lived since their birth, losing their parents to death. But when he arrived in Nabunda, he realized that his watercraft could not travel to their village, Vilma, as the waters were of six feet depth only. And he could not swim. He looked over the large span of waters, saw the village in the distance. He prayed to Mawu Sokpolisa that when there was no hope for man, Mawu Sokpolisa would provide hope. And he was hopeful for hope.

"Granddad returned to the river early at dawn the next morning. Fourteen logs or planks of wood had washed ashore. He pushed one into the river, and, one by one, the third up to the fourteenth, each fifty feet long and joined together, making a seven hundred-foot-long walkway. But it was not sufficient to reach the village. He stepped on the first log, walked its length, and when he was on the second, the first moved swiftly to join the fourteenth log, and the second joined the first, and the same process with the third joining the second after the fourteenth and first, and he reached the village 1380 feet away from the shortest point that he started walking from. The fourteen women who saw what was happening, stood still at the opposite bank and saw coming towards them, a person whose sex they didn't know. He arrived at their side of the banks, and they saw that he looked like their father and must be a man. They all held a calabash of juice and presented it, one after the other, to Granddad. He drank half of whatever quantity was in each calabash, and returned the remaining half to the woman who also drank. He drank half of fourteen.

"The women told him in unison that by his conduct he had married all of them. And that they all had equal ownership in the waters and the land of Nabunda, and by the marriage they had granted to him, and all his children with them and with others forever, the waters and the land.

"Granddad, at dusk, ate with them. And after, he excused them for a while, while they had their baths. And he fell asleep and had a vision of having sexual relations with one of the fourteen women and all fourteen getting pregnant. He felt he had received confirmation from Mawu Sokpolisa that the impossible was going to happen. He slept that night on the island, and as he was having sexual relations with one of them, her moans were like continuous songs in every hut, and it was just like how the logs were joined, their bodies joined by a cord, unseen but felt by the women. After one hour of sexual health celebration or sharing, they slept, and at dawn, the woman who received him into her asked for another session. Granddad yielded and the earlier moans of 'Ahs' and 'Ohs' were replicated. At the first rays of the sun, they set out for Granddad's mansion in the city and country closest to Nabunda, two hundred fifty nautical miles away."

Anna got up from her writing desk and Melon Jnr followed her to find out what she would do. She walked to the bedroom, laid on the bed, and Melon Jnr lay by her and asked, "Was Granddad ever afraid when he was faced with unusual situations?"

"I have also asked him such a question. And also, many other grandchildren who heard his stories of his experiences have asked similar questions. And the answer each time was that Mawu Sokpolisa, the five-names-god, protected and secured him through the five elements in the five names. And that he only had to exercise patience so as not to be ahead of Mawu Sokpolisa's directions or directives," Anna explained.

"Thanks, Anna. Thanks, Mawu Sokpolisa through Granddad. Thanks, Granddad," Melon Jnr said.

CHAPTER 25

Mawu Sopkolisa 's edict: eat the foods of each season

Philadelphia, PA, USA. November 8, 2017

"Granddad didn't ever fall sick or get any disease throughout his life on Earth and that was why he was changed to his heart's desire of the enigmatic tree, consisting of two thousand fruit trees in one tree," Anna said to the husband.

"I ate venison in the mansions of the first wealthy man I worked with. And I ate it in my home with my then wife. Not knowing it was food for the sight and tongue only, but not for the body as a whole and therefore health. Then, I began working with Mr Melon Elembele and ate insects and worms. The lunches at the Elembele's, my first week of working with Granddad, I threw up many times when I got home, but not after I ate venison, to my satisfaction. And I therefore always had excuses not to eat lunch at work with Mr Elembele. But a few weeks before he became Granddad Elembele to me, I knew I would have to copy and practise some things from the Elembele home. My mind often wondered why Mr. Elembele's health statistics and physique was better than mine, a younger man, fifty years younger than him. And I unfortunately 'boasted' of many ailments that took half of my monthly salary because I had to be on medications every day," Melon Jnr said.

"You could have asked Granddad for his secret of good health and for those of his family. His sexual health celebration or sharing was one factor. But the greater and the wisest factor was what he ate and we also ate. I did not ever eat venison, neither him. Not that we as youngsters initially didn't long for it when we set our eyes on it. But we were taught and understood that you don't eat to please your sight and taste buds. Well, you became an Elembele and ate what we ate—"

"But I didn't ever understand why we didn't eat the previous day's food or the past weather season's food (previous season). For, I reckoned that understanding comes to the obedient who is getting a beneficial outcome from an act, and he carries on the act though he doesn't understand but will do it faithfully, the act. And that rewards in multiples," Melon Jnr explained.

"It has taken you too long to know the details and the history behind the family's food tradition. I hope you remember Janus. I spoke about her, the role she played in Granddad's life, the exposure but discipline . . .

"Some time after Granddad's return from the stay with her, he was shown, while asleep, various pages of a writing (a document) that spoke about how to eat, what things to eat, and the relationship between eating those foods and health. And all because he didn't allow sight (eyes) to make him to do what would have been wrong to Janus.

"And it was recorded to his credit that by not failing the sight temptation, he would not fail the taste temptation, hence the later revelation to him as to things to eat, and what time-lines to eat them so that he would be healthy and not die; for good people must not die, but be changed into another form. And he, from then onwards, ate according to what was shown him on the pages. And because he did not want members of his family to die, he not only taught us, but ensured that we followed the words in the document.

"And we ate according to the seasons and what each season yielded in terms of fruits, vegetables, tubers, grains, insects, worms, fishes and crabs. And we have not suffered a famine of anything in any season. The more the family numbers increased and we harvested those various seasonal items, the more they yielded to us, and ceased only when another season began. Fruits according to their seasons. Snails according to their seasons. And when anybody we saw or met was unwell or sick or carried a disease, we knew that the person could not be an Elembele, and has eaten a previous day's food, or a previous season's yield or food, or had eaten what is not in the list. Each fresh season and its yields eaten yields fresh seasons of life. And so how can you be sick or suffer disease and die?" Anna asked.

"Wow! I now fully understand why the daily walk by sisters into the woods, whether it be winter or summer. And at times by their brothers. And the people of the nations in various countries of the world died because of this factor also, for they ate the past in the present and in the future. They stored it. And didn't daily go out walking for only the season's yields. They didn't know anything about our type of eating, because Mawu Sokpolisa didn't sent any one to reveal it to them because they failed the temptation of sight and of taste," Melon Jnr mentioned.

"You are right, as once you fail the temptation of sight, logically and practically you fail that of taste," Anna explained.

CHAPTER 26

Speak to Mawu Sokpolisa and be sensitive

Philadelphia, PA, USA. November 9, 2017

"Granddad had mentioned before the first trip with him to Zamuda that we must speak alone and only to Mawu Sokpolisa. Tell him what is on your heart. And what you wish to achieve and to prosper your ways on the journey and at your destination. And he urged that the traveller be sensitive, because there are territorial spirits in homes or sleeping places and various locations that may wrestle with you not to achieve your intentions," Melon Jnr mentioned to Anna.

"Every step you take on Earth to do anything must be a physical and spiritual step because you will come against physical resistance and spiritual resistance when some humans and their controlling spirits like the status quo and do not want change. Because change means their removal or their dispossessing of what they held. That was what I noticed on visits to places to effect change or development. I suppose you wish to share some of your experiences with me; the experiences would always be different to different persons and I will listen with rapt attention, though I also had many on trips with Granddad," Anna assured him.

"The first night of our arrival was peaceful and serene. I slept deeply, though I thought attacks would be launched that first night to unsettle me, but that didn't happen. A week on, I had let down my guard, and when at night while asleep, four men came to rub some chemical in my hair and it penetrated into my head. It was very smelly. It stank. And they had come from another country, Saaria, to launch the attack at the invitation of the Zamuda people, because strangely they mentioned their country's name.

"I felt unwell in body, my waist was painful, and I could barely stand straight when I awoke in the morning. A person must not be sick or suffer from any disease because of their manner of eating. I struggled to straighten my body to accompany Granddad out. But I noticed that while out of the room, I felt well.

"And for the next five days, while I felt sick in the bedroom, I felt well out of the room. I didn't tell Granddad what was happening. I forgot. Then, a thought came to me that if I went to sleep at a particular named inn, the Zamuda College Inn, I would not feel sick when indoors. At that property, I realized that it was a territorial attack that had been launched against me. I went back to the apartment, took anointing water, and while invoking Mawu Sokpolisa's name, anointed my bedroom, actually all the apartment.

"And I scattered rock salt at the four corners of each room within the apartment, and I was suddenly relieved of the sickness. You know what I remembered? I didn't take authority and control over the apartment by prayer and supplication to Mawu Sokpolisa when I went into my apartment that first day of our arrival. And when I did, at that later stage, Mawu Sokpolisa sent four angels who walked with me, and even were with me in the washroom or restroom. And if anyone should ask how I knew that four angels were with me . . . I saw them. They were in the form of my image and took on my likeness. After another week, and praying daily invoking the name of Mawu Sokpolisa to be a protective cover every day, Granddad and I travelled five hundred miles further into the interior of Zamuda.

"We were again in different apartments. This time, on being given the keys, I prayed over the keys that the apartment and the rooms that they open into would be filled with the presence of Mawu Sokpolisa, for only Mawu Sopkolisa can dwell in every room. but I, one at a time. I didn't realize that Mawu Sokpolisa sometimes withdraws the awesome protective presence to test you as to whether, when the enemies attack at any time, you will call on Mawu Sokpolisa.

"On the fifth day, we went to many places in the town centre, met and chatted with them, and asked questions that made some to know that we were first-time visitors. And they were honest and sincere in their answers to us, knowing that we were no spies that would see the weakness of their places and come to destroy them as were wont in those times.

"A few women touched my body while answering my questions. I didn't pray against such touching, because in my mind they meant well. But I was mistaken. For at night, in a dream, I had the same women touching various parts of my body, and again I felt it was just polite and warm for a visitor to allow the residents to show the warmness of their culture to you. But one by one, each made an attempt to pull off my pyjamas, and when I protested, then each became angry that they were warm during the daytime hours to me so that at night I would also show warmth of a man to them. And they further explained that visitors to their land are gods who must be married through mating with them – the women. And on the gods' departure to their destination, the gods will remember that you gave of yourself to them, and will be under reciprocal obligation to send you gifts.

"When I heard their explanation, I knew I was under their cultural obligation, (we were within their land and their cultural norms must apply), and could not revoke a contract that each entered into with me during the day and for a reciprocity at night in the form of sexual relations. (I will not mention sexual health celebration or sharing since I don't know what they believe about sexual relations between a man and a woman or between a woman and a god.)

"Each gave me five minutes to consider and therefore do what was expected, otherwise they would make a report to their judicial authorities to come and arrest me that night and charge me. Not wanting to suffer imprisonment in a foreign land, I asked each of them to allow me to go to the bathroom to freshen up. But while in the bathroom alone, door closed, I prayed with fervency saying, 'Mawu Sokpolisa, I don't want to be an adulterer. They are not of the Melon Elembele family, and share not my beliefs as your adherent. Deliver, by coming to my rescue.'

"I then heard the thunders and saw the lightning flashes as Mawu Sokpolisa was wont to do when we call upon it and it answers.

"'Thank you Mawu Sokpolisa,' I said in that bathroom before stepping out to face the women. But they were all gone. The next day I informed Granddad of what happened at night. He only said, and I am quoting his words, 'The rites of passage are gone through in the physical world. And you must go through rites of passage in the spiritual world also. But, it is unending. It may come every day and as many times as in Sokpolisa 2 verse 7 of five times. And as you said, you cried to Mawu Sokpolisa, so will Mawu Sokpolisa hear your dependent cry and rescue you.'

"So, now that I have mentioned part of his words 'of dependent cry', could there also be a non-dependent cry?" Melon Jnr asked.

"Why not? When your desire for something outweighs your cry of deliverance from it. In the spirit world, your words are weighed to determine your true intent. If your desire is to have sexual relations with a married woman (a woman married to another man), and that desire or wish arises in you for days on end, and or months on end, and she bedecks her bed for you, and cries for you, then to Mawu Sokpolisa will be a 'dependent' cry to deliver you, for the desires of those many days or months though unspoken words would be weightier than the cry for deliverance. But Mawu Sokpolisa delivers even with inconsistent or broken desires or 'on and off' desires," Anna explained.

"Mawu Sokpolisa is two times kind to us to deliver. But only one time not to deliver," Melon said.

While Anna again said, "As Granddad said, I am adding in the rites of passage in the spiritual realm, even the chapels whose doors you enter should put red warning flashes in your heart, homes you enter, offices, gifts, and people you associate with and many others.

"Pray that Mawu Sokpolisa will keep you safe always. But don't despise those who are trapped. They will have been caught in the snare by other people's culture or traditions. Pray for these also. When they are redeemed, you have more brothers and sisters to shout the songs of all families redeemed," Anna advised.

CHAPTER 27

What the seventy twin daughters of Zurion taught the Melon Elembele family

Philadelphia, PA, USA. November 10, 2017

"Granddad Melon Elembele thought we were the brightest and best and with the highest IQs on Earth and in the heavens and under the seas. Then he heard of the seventy twin daughters of Zurion who lived with their parents under the seas, then aged between three years and fifty-five years. Granddad was one who could traverse any part of the universe to see what exceptional things or beings Mawu Sokpolisa had done or created that he was not aware of. He did that so that if they were more wondrous and excellent than his family, he could appreciate them and express gratitude to Mawu Sokpolisa for such wonderful or awesome beings. And if not as wonderful as the Melon Elembele family, also praise Mawu Sokpolisa for the heights they, the Melon Elembele family, had attained, but also seek and desire humility in each member, so as not to feel superior to others.

"Their sprawling home under the seas was not difficult to find because of the sheer architectural beauty. All the buildings were covered with more than ten thousand shells of diverse kinds. And pools of water fell from the middle portion of each of the seventy-two buildings like waterfalls at the rising of the sun and at sunset. When the sun set, the children, each twin, carried out brain exercises to come up with something new every night before they fell asleep, so that the following morning, the new thing by each twin would be introduced and therefore seventy new things were introduced every day as part of their life. And that is seventy new inventions each day. Their parents were so awed that they stayed away from their children, not wishing to be found wanting in many ways, since even the three-year-old children carried IQs of eighty-year-olds of the past century.

"Their mum occasionally visited them in the evenings, not to scold them, for they did nothing wrong ever, but simply to fan her admiration at daughters who came out of her womb with such amazing talents.

"When Granddad and seventy of us arrived to observe them from a far, we were older than them all, fifty times, but we didn't, seventy of us Melon Elembele family members, do one millionth of what we saw they had done or will do. After one month under the sea observing at the end of each day, we had no doubts in our minds that there were others wiser and more intelligent, and no person in the universe should be proud when it has not seen what things or other people are dwelling elsewhere and what they did or are doing. Granddad told us that when you are amazed at something, there is an awesome Mawu Sokpolisa behind it, therefore praise and honour Mawu Sokpolisa. While in the past, that is before our setting eyes on and hearing the seventy twin daughters of Zurion, we celebrated praise and honour of Mawu Sokpolisa once every month. But after seeing them, we changed that to a weekly event.

"A time came, two years later, when Granddad heard and saw through a special mirror he had that gave him sight and audio of everything under the sea, and he found that the seventy twin children had invited their parents to a meeting and informed them that they would no longer call them 'Mum' and 'Dad', because the fishes under the sea found their parents so stupid that they always laughed at them, the children. And not only that, the fishes called them not by their individual names that they knew, but rather, 'the children of the stupid mother and father'.

"We will no more have reproach if we mention that we are the children of a god and a goddess whose dwelling is in the skies and gave birth to us, but engaged you as maiden of honour and gentleman of honour to look after us when we decided to live under the sea, because we were excited by the myriad things under the seas while the heavens gave only twinkling stars.

"But their mum and dad didn't understand what they, the children, meant by what they said. As to whether the children were disowning them as mother and father or just simply stating a truth, because it is a god and goddess who give children. And the mum and dad were unsure, unable to ask for explanation because they feared to be mocked by their own children because of their level of intelligence. So, they told the children that it was true, that it is a god and goddess that gave children, and a mum and a dad are just caretakers or stewards and therefore they were at liberty to tell the fishes that truth so that the fishes would stop calling them by reference to a stupid mother and father. The children jubilated at the words of the 'caretakers'. And so, the children informed the fishes that a god and a goddess were their parents, just like the fishes under the sea. And like the fishes, each known by its name, they became known by their individual names again.

"Some years passed, and a great animal, Bugatti, fell into the waters and established its dwelling under the sea. It traversed under the seas from north to south and east to west, looking for any living thing under the seas that didn't have parents for its meal. For such must not dwell under the seas. The fishes pointed to their parents, their likeness and image. They were therefore spared, not eaten. The seventy twin children could not point to any parents, adults in whose images and likeness they were made. Bugatti therefore ate them all.

"Granddad was saddened to hear of their destruction when his mirror related events to him. We were equally saddened, especially the seventy of us that saw and heard them at sunsets doing brain exercises.

"And without Granddad telling us the lesson to learn from the seventy twin daughters of Zurion, we said we will not disown a mother or a father, whether wise, clever or stupid. They provide parental cover nevertheless, and its blessings are not today but futuristic," Anna said.

While Melon Jnr said, "Even the vulture has a mum and dad," but quickly apologized saying, "Everything is peculiarly beautiful in creation."

"I would have skinned you alive or asked for your removal from the family. Some members of the Melon Elembele family were and are vultures. Remember the calling of names of grandchildren and their turning into various animals that day," Anna said.

CHAPTER 28

My speaking, my prison

Philadelphia, PA, USA. November 11, 2017

"Some countries are no-go areas for some. If you love liberty, free speech subject only to the laws of defamation and sedition, then there are many countries not to visit on Earth. Not that there are cannibals in those countries to eat your flesh after drinking your blood. But your opened mouth (without the entry of houseflies) that speaks could land you in jail when the person next to you said your spoken words were not 'sweet' to his or her ears, or you have put him or her or the sexless in fear of injury, death or hell by your spoken words. The test is subjective, not objective. Once the person accuses you, you must spend twelve months of jail time in a prison or a dungeon, where you will be taught, through whipping with the cane, not to speak outdoors in politically incorrect language, but inside your room. I am afraid to say that in ten countries and counting, the domestic or home environment has not been excluded from the application of the law," Anna mentioned to her husband after dinner.

"Hi, sweetheart. Some stories are not bedtime stories. It is not only children of under ten years that need bedtime stories to fall asleep. But grown-ups also need bedtime stories, the romantic type, for the sizzling times and deep sleep thereafter. If your words would make me not touch you for passion and deep sleep, then that also must be a crime to lead to imprisonment for six months. Eh! If there is no such law as yet, I hereby pass it as 'words stultifying romance or prohibiting it are not allowed at

101

bedtime'. The bedroom must be only for language that promotes sexual health celebration or sharing and total wellbeing—"

Anna interjected by saying, "If a husband will not listen to the wife on a matter, tearing her heart apart, and therefore suture her heart with a thread and a balm, then such a husband must be deemed to be in desertion, and the wife can divorce him by saying the words, 'I don't love you' three times to his hearing, and the marriage will end, and another man (taken from the highways) can have the woman that same night as a wife. And the divorced husband must observe whatever will go on between the ex-wife and the 'highway-chosen' man. And I have passed such a law. And it takes immediate effect," Anna said.

"I was only joking. No husband would have the courage to pass such a law. Because it is only women who have the awesome gift that gives forever memories. I hereby revoke the law of my thoughts and of my lips with effect from when the first word of the law was spoken," Melon Jnr assured.

"My retelling of the events will have a romantic end, and sexual health celebration or sharing beginning. Because a wife who is in love and wishes to have her husband to always cherish her knows how to weave words to achieve that end," Anna said.

"I am assured, because when it is the woman giving, she gives all her fullness without any reservations. But when it is the man taking, he is unable to take her fullness. I am expectant and will look for the symbolism," Melon Jnr expressed.

"My Granddad would go where the door was closed, and would open and make entry into the room. And when he heard and confirmed the number of countries with such laws, he said we could go and break the law and there would be no conviction for us to entail imprisonment. With twenty countries to visit, (countries without the Melon brand), he booked hotels for us in the city centres where the largest gathering of people would be. He assured the granddaughter, Protect, and me that we would be under the fire of protection always. And that, that fire, is also a fire of defence: attack.

"When we arrived in the first country, there was a milling crowd in the city centre. Though they were celebrating a festival, no one was speaking or singing songs because of the law of political correctness in speech and song. They had each a green leaf in their mouth, but they were only drumming. But I wondered in my mind if the drum language could also not breach the law. And as Granddad was hurrying us up to get to the hotel, and I asked Protect (who was next to me) if she understood drum language. She answered yes, and explained that there were as many drum languages as a drummer would play. And unlike a human being who could speak a number of languages she knew, a drummer possessed by a spirit could drum as many languages as the spirit could trigger in him. When she gave her explanation, I thought whether it could be a defence when charged with breach of the political correctness law, to plead spirit possession and therefore the spirit spoke.

"We were at the hotel reception, filling in personal details to check in, when two policemen came to affect our arrest for speaking words that breached the political correctness law. Granddad asked them to state what exactly we said that breached the law. To Granddad's question, we saw that they were unable to speak. Granddad repeated his question. We felt, Protect and I, that they didn't hear Granddad's questions.

"The receptionist, uncertain as to what was happening, called the hotel security who took the two policemen into their car. They were still not saying anything, so hotel security called the emergency services, and two vehicles came over and took them to the hospital – so we were informed by the security when they came back and asked Granddad what the matter was. He told them of the intended arrest. They brushed the whole issue aside and returned to their sentry posts.

"We ate lunch and went back to the city centre, conversing loudly enough to be heard. And with no more threat of arrest, we decided to take a ride in cab. And when the cabbie came, he sympathetically said it was a sad day in the city because all the festival celebrants, by refusing to speak or sing, had all gone deaf and dumb. He told us further that he believed in spiritual things. And that the god who gave humans the power of speaking and hearing, and who had been offended by the refusal to speak or sing, had taken away those two powers or abilities. He expressed the premonition that as night follows day, the legislators also were bound to suffer similar fate soon.

"We were in the fourth country, when he sent a message to Granddad's number that the legislators had all suffered a similar fate as the festival goers.

"Granddad then asked that we don't rejoice at what was happening across countries with their people becoming deaf and dumb. We hearkened to his words. And so, legislators in twenty countries have come under a 'curse' – what the newspapers called the 'curse of physicians' who had lost earnings as a result of very few falling sick and going to clinics and, therefore, people falling sick of deafness and dumbness was good omen for physicians.

"When Protect asked Granddad as to what was next for the legislators, Granddad explained that they will retire, unless someone could make a device or gadget that could hear and also speak to be used by them. But theirs being god- or spirit-inflicted, any device made will not avail them. And no others will be willing to take their place.

"We have all our five senses intact, moreover the trigger senses . . ."

Anna didn't complete her sentence. And the husband tickled her on the upper arm.

Anna then said, "It is good to have all your senses. And no threat of imprisonment because of the use of any. That is our humanity."

CHAPTER 29

Everyone a worker in Melon Elembele family

Jacksonville, FLA, USA. November 12, 2017

"When I see some on various trips, either with Granddad or alone, of the people of the nations in the various countries of the world saying they are unemployed, it shocks me to the core. They are idlers, sitting at one place, or roaming about doing nothing with their hands, their feet, their mouths, nostrils, taste buds, heads. Not using any part of their body, I ask, what is the difference? How is it that in the Melon Elembele family, the sun rises for more than twelve hours in the tropical parts, but each person does what he must do. And for the temperate countries, whether the sun rises or not, child or adult must do its portion of work till the evening (closing) hours, except for breaks and meal times. And for our twenty-four-hour operations, the cycle breaks not," Anna mentioned to a group of select family members from age four who must be taught that everyone a worker is.

"And what did Granddad do to get each to work?" Anna asked.

But she didn't expect the children to answer, though many hands went up. And instead of the question posed being answered, she then asked, "What will you do to occupy your day, meaningfully?"

Little Leticia spoke as follows: "On waking up I brush my teeth, take my bath, then eat breakfast, then I go back to tidy my bed and room. I help my mummy with things in the kitchen, all within timelines fixed. I then leave for the Melon Elembele school for youngsters. While at school, we are given empty cereal boxes and told to craft whatever we wish to craft, and that after learning the letters of the alphabet or numbers. Today I cut and folded my cereal box into letter Z and W and the number 7, because we had the previous week learnt about numbers.

"Two hours later, we change into sports attire and go out to play paired games. That takes an hour. Then a shower we take, dress again and eat a mid-morning snack. Ten minutes are allowed for thinking over all that happened till the mid-morning snack, or to go to the restroom. After washing our hands with water and soap and mopping with paper towels that are disposed of in the recycling bin, but not thrown on the floor, we go back to classes, where, for another two hours, each take a turn to say what somebody has done with a cereal box that caught your imagination and why. After that session, a final session is held for us to think of what we will do to help or make Mummy happy when we get home or when she gets home later.

"I will sing the song we learn. Or I will tell about how useful cereal boxes are and should not be thrown away to make a big fireball – but only after we children have cut them into various bits and pieces, crafting or making numbers or alphabets, or animals or birds, whatever we learnt the previous week.

"When classes end for the day at 3:00 pm, and after a siesta of thirty minutes, we wake up to eat a meal and help to put things in the dishwasher or share lessons learned at school until Mummy gets back from work – formal work outside the home or as a homemaker worker shares stories of her day with us four-year-olds.

"And that is one day, and each such one day is replicated till we are sixteen, when we must spend our vacations in factories and malls, just to mention two. And when we turn eighteen years, we must work and also attend college. And there is place for everyone. The one who sings goes to the factory to sing to the workers on the factory floor. The poet writing poems about the beauty and usefulness of work recites it to workers to encourage them to do more. We blend all the talents and achieve maximum results as embossed on machines by the manufacturer – a Melon Elembele, or as each human is capable to achieve."

And when Leticia was done, others had their turn as to what they do every day. That was what Granddad introduced many years earlier: catching them young, introducing them to the value of work as beneficial to them and the family. And they all choosing what they are capable of doing and fitting, and together achieving results.

Anna closed the session at the day's end satisfied that what Granddad started had not been lost with time but was safely being carried out. Everyone a worker, and all workers in Melon Elembele family.

CHAPTER 30

Some of our travel experiences across nations

Jacksonville, FL, USA. November 12, 2017

"It was during the beginning of the expansion of the Melon brand into various countries of the people of the nations, that we arrived in the first country on the twenty-countries tour, expecting nothing unusual. Granddad had purchased land and acquired equipment, including vehicles, in all those countries. And he had an invitation signed by the various commerce and industry secretaries in each country. And not a man amenable to diplomatic niceties, he declined such treatment and explained further that he would want his grandchildren to experience the world as everybody else, not like the 'exclusives' who know not the world or understand it because from birth they made themselves the ruling class or associates of the ruling class.

"I had hoped that one day he would oblige us to be exposed to the world of diplomacy also. But he explained to us that those who experience and leave in that world tend to forget that it is unreal. It is fleeting and ends when he that made you a diplomat says no more because it was your time to move backwards. And not having known the real world, you are confused as to what the world is and you will be forever bitter that you were not treated well. Nobody ever refused to go along with Granddad on any matter without an explanation, moreover when he offered an explanation.

"Hmm! Melon Jnr, I took you on a detour. But that offers you what my mind did on the journeys sometimes with Granddad and others. Granddad didn't ever travel those days without his

Alsatian dog by his side. And when we disembarked, he was followed by Vanguard, that was his dog's name. We walked briskly through immigration as we carried passports of the country of arrival. But we were stopped at the customs and preventive post. A woman insisted on searching our carry-on bags and expressed anger (she was wild-eyed and the few seconds she took to make the demand, her eyes had turned blood-red) that we had no checked-in luggage. I didn't understand the import of her anger. What the checked-in luggage would have done to or for her, had we arrived with such, we couldn't tell.

"Granddad had always warned us before any trip not to ever challenge or quote a law to customs and preventive staff. They detest it. Their eyes see much good and great stuff coming in and going out; things they desire like many others to own but will not own because they don't earn many millions, and therefore allow envy to blind them so that their minds can't look behind their eye to see how to get it. Oh! Again, I have gone on a detour. I am a woman and I offer details so that you can go through the maze of deserts or rivers, or mountain peaks or deep valleys.

"We opened our carry-on bags. But she directed that they be placed on a raised granite platform. We did. Somehow something from my hand luggage got attached to her wedding band. It turned out to be a (50ml) small bottle of perfume, the 'Rosarisa' brand. I don't know whether she saw and knew what had happened. And she asked that we close our bags and move out through the exit.

"And as she turned to walk away, Vanguard jumped on her and wouldn't let go. Five officers rushed to her aid. Vanguard let go of her and she fell on her back. He then pushed against one of the other five and, when he was falling, he fell against another who fell against another and all five were on the floor. Vanguard went to the woman and with both front paws lifted her to sitting position. The perfume bottle was visible for others to see. And when some other officer came walking over with two dogs, he didn't speak before the two dogs went near the customs and preventive officer and smelt the perfume stuck in her wedding band and barked loudly.

"I didn't know what that meant. As I don't understand the language of every dog. But that of Vanguard I know because I live in the same houses with him. Oh! With the evidence on her wedding band, we followed her and the officer to an office ten feet away. A while later, a medical emergency crew came and carried the other five away. Possibly they were seriously injured when they fell against each other and onto the hard granite floor.

"The other officer introduced himself as Bolita, the command officer. He apologized for what had happened. And he asked Granddad if he wanted further disciplinary measures to be taken against the officer apart from the outright dismissal she would suffer. Granddad explained that that was unnecessary, as the scars on the officer would be a reminder to her that she that harbours suspicions on most travellers, and seeks confirmation to affect an arrest instead of good wishes or well wishes for travellers who would become a ransom for the innocents.

"'I have always told them to have a good conscience towards all who walk through our entry points, otherwise our evil thoughts will be our own undoing,' he said. 'I thank you, sir. You will receive a letter in the post within the next twenty-four hours. Your Alsatian dog and ours are more disciplined than the human beings. They zero in on the one guilty out of the millions of travellers who come through the airport. I am sorry that the future is dogs but not humans, because technology I abhor. May I please keep my reasons personal because in saying it I could be a target for a hit man or woman', the command officer said.

"Granddad shook his hand as Bolita asked whether he could pat our shoulders, the two of us women. But Granddad made us stretch our hands to shake his, while explaining that apart from women accusing of sexual harassment, men also do it when it suits them or serves their selfish interests well.

"We were able to do everything in this country. On our way out to the airport to fly out, the country's commerce and industry secretary telephoned Granddad to state that Granddad failed to tell him of what had happened at the customs and preventive post on our arrival. Granddad apologized for that oversight. And the secretary also apologized for the incident, but said, "The secretary in charge of the department has reviewed procedures to detail only dogs at the busiest airports.

"'How sad! Humans are displacing themselves for what are not humans, while we take the nature of the cat to take the fried chicken portions that doesn't belong to us,' I heard Granddad respond.

"A few hours later, we were in another airport but in another country. We went for dinner after checking into our hotel. When the first course was served of soup, Vanguard pushed all three soup bowls into one corner of the square table we sat at: the language of Vanguard at work. None of us took the soup, though we paid for it. The second and third courses Vanguard was excited about. And we ate to our fill and went back to our hotel. Next day, ten malls were opened by Granddad, and assisted by the two of us, the granddaughters he was then doting upon. Oh, just in case you are wondering where Vanguard was, he was the faithful fourth assistant of Granddad but ahead of us all in understandings of things in nature.

"We spent only two days in this country. In country three, the immigration queue was longer than the terminal building, and they gave us numbers and asked that we sit on the benches provided for seating. It took three hours to go through immigration. But Granddad didn't care a hoot as to the number of hours, and he explained, 'In life, be prepared for all eventualities and take no shortcuts, for there is a time for everything under sun or on Earth. And each thing you go through ensures that you go through everything in time as challenges, so you can at its end, say I achieved what was ordained for me.'

"We stayed in a guest house. But each time we stepped out of the house, we returned bubbling with energy and excitement. But once inside the three-bedroom guest house, there was heaviness and sorrow in our hearts. Granddad mentioned it. And so also my sister Ella. Vanguard didn't play with us and looked distant from us as if he knew or had a premonition of our soon death, and was therefore mourning our death and the loneliness to come. Sleep wasn't easy either. And we couldn't explain the unusual tremors in our limbs at night.

"Granddad, to our mind, knew it was an evil spirit left by a woman to cause discomfort to us so that we would leave the guest house so she could have her permanent habitation there, and it would be one of the uninhabited buildings by humans but a spirit. And therefore, while at dinner in the dining room, Granddad said, 'Mawu Sokpolisa, wherever we stay, is your habitation. And it is your spirit that must dwell in. All other spirits flee.'

"At the word 'flee', Vanguard rubbed against each of us in turn, starting from Ella, then Granddad and me. And our remaining twelve days were of warmth and wellbeing inside the guest house and not only outside it.

"We were transiting through a big airport to leave our aircraft and hire a smaller aircraft to an airstrip and drive in a vehicle to our destination and had to go through security. A young woman in her early twenties lifted Granddad's hand luggage and shouted, 'Whose is this?' And without waiting for answer, opened the zip and not flipped through, but jumbled and tumbled his few things – underwear and shirts – leaving them looking as if they were not iron-pressed. She then ordered, 'Repack your belongings, you are through.'

"When I heard the rude manner with which she spoke, I wondered whether they were trained or what made them so rude. She didn't 'wear' a smile that would invite anyone to compliment her on a good job done. Vanguard rushed to repack the things, as Ella and I knew she wouldn't allow us to repack, for we heard her say that no other person could help you, even if you are infirm or disabled. She shouted at Vanguard asking, 'Are you a human being? And have I searched you?' At her second question, Vanguard pounced on her ears, pulling both ears with its paws. Two officers next to her involuntarily fled. Others stood dumbfounded. She cried to be released because of the pain in her ears, and said, 'I sincerely apologize.' And Vanguard let go. She then saluted as if Granddad was the commandant. But he didn't look her at face to see what she did. And we didn't move one step, before a whole platoon of security officers came as if invaders had invaded.

"'Please, sir, your guard dog had committed a crime and we must take him into custody,' said a woman whose stripes looked like the most senior among them. 'If he is my guard dog and you are taking him into custody, then I must also go into custody with him. He did no wrong. He only taught your junior officer not to be rude in her service to people. When a human being doesn't behave properly and no other human can reprimand or correct her conduct, a well-trained animal will discipline her,' Granddad explained.

"The senior-looking officer, said, 'It was wrong for a dog to find her guilty and impose a penalty on her. She should have been taken to court in accordance with our constitution.'

"'My response, officer, is that the dog only reprimanded her. As for court, I will make a report on her conduct. And yours also–' Without Granddad completing his sentence, she interjected by saying, 'Nothing was heard by me, but my ears hurt. Eh! They are so painful.' She was whisked away. While the rude officer said, 'Please let them go. Please, I would like to work for you. If you can train a dog that well, then I will receive training from you so that I will not be dispensed with and replaced by intelligent animals. I see that time coming. It is only two years away.'

"'Another family member,' I murmured to Ella. And as if Granddad heard me, he said, 'You could join us on our journey to Malevin.'

"I am walking out of this job – a job where you are taught to see all others as criminals when we, the gatekeepers, pinch things from luggage, many not knowing that some things have been removed until many weeks later.'

Vanguard patted her on her lower lips with his right paw, as she said, 'This is more than the love of man.' Because of Vanguard's conduct, we felt compelled to hug her. And the security officers and other travellers watched all that happened patiently, because nobody raised a voice of complaint.

"Could it be that they thought that a certain god had come through their airport with its two daughters and a dog, and whoever raised a complaint would have suffered some malady? Hubby, don't answer me. I see a future with that. No more humans coming to attack, but spirits or gods to discipline humans and correct them and animals posted as security," Anna said.

While Melon Jnr in response said, "It will be awesome when your ears are being pulled by something, but you don't recognize because you can't see and recognize. Exciting times lie ahead of those who want to ride others roughshod but can't be punished because lawlessness by security will be the norm. I will be traveling with you then as Granddad also did with you. A past of travels and so also a future of travels. We are writing down the past and we can compare it with the present and also with the future."

"We departed for the next stage of our countries tour. The airstrip was the size of one wingspan of our aircraft, the 747: 970 series. Granddad disembarked with Vanguard, followed by Ziina, the security officer. Ella and I immediately followed her so that she could chat with us and us with her. Ziina was surprised that passengers had to go through security to enter the small town. And knowing how they behave, and not knowing whether the others had communicated to her colleagues at other airports that she was no more one of them, (not that she expected any waivers for her), she walked fast and stood next to Granddad and we joined two minutes later. Granddad mentioned that we were a Granddad and family on a visit to the first officer of the line-up of seven security officers, who asked if there was anything to declare, please, with a smile. 'No,' Granddad said. 'Then follow the green-marked walkway,' she answered.

"I am feeling tired. Maybe I should tell you what happened on entry into other countries of the people of the nations' airports?" Anna suggested.

"Yeah, that is fine. But I am itching to know about any particular behaviour or attitude of Ziina," said Melon Jnr.

"Eh! Again Eh! If she were carrying a gun she would have killed some of the security officers at four of the return journey airports. They were rude, like her, especially the women when they had the power to put you, a traveller, behind bars because they think you are fortunate or rich enough to travel across the countries of the people of the nations, then they proudly display their power. But she had no gun. And Vanguard did not act the way he did to her.

"At the first family meeting on our return, she told Granddad that had she have been taught to place herself in the traveller's position of an innocent traveller visiting to admire nature in its varied forms in other countries, her behaviour and language would have been different. But she had learnt through practice, and explained that she now understood the traveller. 'I would recommend role-modelling this type of training for service professions, especially security-related professions, because powers of arrest and jailing goes into their mind and they think they are above all other humans and professions. And if you think you are above all, then the animals are the future, even flies or insects will teach humans what we should have known through proper training,' Ziina had concluded, and her quote was made known to me by another sister."

CHAPTER 31

The travel experiences of five more flights to five countries

Jacksonville, FL, USA. November 13, 2017

"My husband, the day is chilly today. But your presence around me will make me feel warm. And I intend to continue from where I left off yesterday.

"And, as you may recall, there was a new family member in the making, awaiting adoption to be a fully-fledged member. The other day, I didn't mention to you that she wrote a two-paragraph note to her elderly parents of living her life with another family before our departure with her. And she accompanied us on the flight to the sixth country of the people of the nations in the various countries of the world, and knowing Granddad and how he did things of learning through exposure to experiences, she was part of our team to four countries.

"Ziina was taller than Ella and me. And when walking with us she walked in the middle, and the three of us arranged as Ella, Ziina and Anna, the shape of what we three girls called the 'EZA' or the pyramid. And when we arrived in the sixth country we walked majestically, though not royals or laying claim to that, towards the customs and preventive post, and all eyes were on us, the men possibly saying in their hearts, 'What awesome, beautiful girls to have in their home, to be the best garden of women to ever have walked on Earth.' And, again this is only a presumption, while the women were saying, 'Those three women are trophy wives of the elderly man walking ahead of them with his dog, and will not be competitors with us as to have access to our husbands, if the men or husbands should set eyes on them.' I even conjectured that the women may alternatively say that, 'The way they are so beautiful and charming, they are gods that go through certain airports once to show off their splendour and are seen no more. Their appearance at the particular airport to only remind women who live on Earth that there are women in other realms who come to only observe how we look like, and how different they are from them, and go back to live in their own realm. For, is it not truth that an eagle on no account will live on the ground among chicken, but in the heavens above the clouds, their rightful dwelling?'

"Granddad waited for us at the customs point. The customs officers, all eight, smiled at us girls above the height of Granddad. But we didn't by their smile expect to walk through customs unchecked. They asked to check our suitcases. And so, five of them took our luggage off each one of us. I hope you have not forgotten the fifth passenger and our ever-faithful companion?" Anna said and paused.

"Eh! Luggage for a fifth passenger and companion every time?" Melon Jnr asked. After two minutes, he said, 'Oh, you mean Vanguard?"

"There were biscuits or crackers in each carry-on case, in addition to toiletries and underwear for us. They all five said, 'The crackers are in commercial quantities and will be seized and dumped in the trash.' But one of them quickly said, 'You could eat the extra crackers so that it doesn't become waste or trash?' The seven others nodded their heads in approval. While another said to Granddad, 'You have admirable trophy wives. You could buy some more crackers for them when you enter our state?'

"'I am able to do that. But may I please know what the law limits are as to the number of crackers between one state and another in a federation?' Granddad asked. 'It is our discretion to impose limits or not. And we have imposed limits. But I have been kind enough to allow you to eat some instead of dumping them in the trash,' the man who made that suggestion said.

"Granddad asked that we be provided with chairs and bottles of water so we could do as he has suggested. Vanguard was given Granddad's crackers and he ate all. Then it ate his own crackers. A shrill voice sounded loud from the opposite direction to us. We looked, and the officer who suggested eating looked nine months pregnant. The other seven at that post, not knowing what was happening, fled, leaving him. Ziina handed over her twelve packets to Vanguard, who ate them all, and the officer, possibly unable to breathe because he overate, collapsed. We heard of his death some hours later when we were settled in our hotel rooms, because he didn't get medical assistance early enough to make him vomit the excessive crackers.

"Ziina was saddened for a while, saying it could have been her. But she regained her jovial disposition and said to us two girls that when the law was interpreted like it is an ass, the one interpreting makes an ass of himself and becomes a victim of himself, not of the law.

"We stayed two other days in that country and then we were airborne to the seventh country, expecting nothing untoward. But I was wrong. The chauffeur who took us to the hotel, after Granddad had paid with his card, didn't return the card but insisted he did when all five of us saw him put the card his wallet. We asked him to go, but the next morning he was standing at the spot where he stood to process the credit card payment. He looked sunken in his spirit because the warmth he had on his face when he picked us up initially was all gone. And when we returned from the town centre and spent another night at the hotel, he was still standing still and, while leaving the hotel the next morning for departure, he looked dehydrated.

"We girls wondered why none of the hotel staff had seen him in his position for that many days so as to rescue him. But we realized that whatever had arrested him, had caused others not to take notice of him. A year later when we checked into that hotel again, we noticed a monument, not to his memory but a monument that had words: 'Uprightness to known and unknown – the mark of NEELOM HOTEL.'

"We visited an eighth country of the people of the nations without any mishap or wrong act by any. However, on our return, we had to go through security. We carried own non-allergen hand gloves for them to use to search us, because research carried by the top two universities on hand gloves and searches disclosed that the security used the same hand gloves for as many passengers as each searched, and thereby they infected some passengers. And some of them knew that fact. As for cold bacteria, millions had been infected because the bacteria were introduced to the clothing of persons searched, and when you touch the surface of your clothing and your hands go near your nose, mouth or eyes you, in forty-eight hours, go down with the disease. The researchers called it 'The security grown and dispersed diseases'.

"They refused to use our non-allergen hand gloves on the pretext that it would conceal contraband we were carrying, even when it was the same make of gloves (but allergen type) that they used, but multiple times and throughout duty time.

"Vanguard jumped at the officer who refused our request, and tore his hand gloves, forcing him to take a fresh pack, and for each of us, he took a fresh pack. A month later, that airport was closed by civil aviation authorities for causing a pandemic of a deadly type of flu, because passengers who travelled through that airport were all affected. But we were free of the disease. The officer and many others were dismissed as employees as the airport didn't reopen after the initial closure.

"Our trip to a ninth country and a tenth country brought us face to face with the same challenge. The scanners for searches were causing cancer because of manufacturing defect. But some of the operating staff would look at some passengers and decide that they should not live anymore and expose such to more radiation waves than the body could take. Passengers complained of nerve and muscle pains two days after returning from flights.

And some whitish substance also developed in their brains. The blame was put at doorstep of cell phone use.

"And not wanting to be victims, (the particular airports didn't like women travellers), Ella, Ziina and me were in a queue with thousands of male passengers. We asked for manual. Oh! There were no women security officers on duty, so we thought. But it turned out that they don't have women security officers. Not that a woman who decides not to be professional can't do what she is not expected to do. Ziina went forward to be searched manually, but she was asked to walk through the scanner to the scanner exit point and, when she did, there was an explosion and the two officers who stood near the scanner had severe burns, and so also the person operating the scanner. An alarm sounded as other security officers waved us all (including other passengers) to rush into the main terminal building."

"That was ransom for the Melon Elembele family members," Melon Jnr said.

"We have since that day prayed that others would be given as ransoms for us if they desired our injury or death," Anna said.

"That is fairness by Mawu Sokpolisa, and by other gods or goddesses. Do good to others, when you desire such. And failing that, you pay the price of blood or death," Melon Jnr again said.

CHAPTER 32

Granddad convinces on security hand touches and sudden ill health

Jacksonville, FL, USA. November 14, 2017

"Whose fingers would you desire to rub against your body at security check points across countries of the people of the nations?" Anna asked the husband.

"I haven't thought of that ever. But, as a man, I'd love a charming and smiling woman's fingers to rub against or touch my body for warm sensations. And, as a husband, I would want my wife's fingers to explore my body for that contraband which no passenger carries but the passenger 'they – the institution' have put up. And anyway, pretty and attractive and attracting Anna, why worry about fingers of people you don't know touching you for at most five minutes and on the way to your flight you board?" Melon Jnr dismissively said.

"Who touches me even for a minute, not accidentally but purposely or planned, is a bigger worry than walking through an X-ray machine that gives your body ultraviolet rays; but a man or woman whose fingers touch your body in the name of a search and 'inserts' into your body or being two things . . ."

"Sure? Then how come the top three universities have not made a study of that to persuade the authorities in the countries of the people of the nations to adopt a no-touch policy by fingers of X to the body of Y?' Melon Jnr asked.

"My husband, why do you prefer the fingers of a charming woman (I call her 'sizzler') to touch or rub your body? And even that she must have a smile on her face to radiate warmth into you? And again, why would you prefer Anna's fingers to rub or touch your body, to hers? The answer was in your sentence about the preferences. But you, like the three universities, have lost it. I will tell you of what Granddad did: Granddad provided funding to those three universities (of the people of the nations) to carry out a study. They were not the Melon Elembele family universities.

"Granddad met ten secretaries in charge of airport security and the aviation matters of ten advanced countries of the people of the nations on his Vota island, because they heard that aircraft that landed on that island were converted and filled with a one-time gas: lepoid. But it, when mixed with carbon dioxide coming from inside the aircraft, propelled the aircraft throughout its lifespan. Additionally, Granddad had a secret that went beyond the aircraft's lifespan.

"You know, Granddad is charming and warm with his unforgettable smile. He gave each arriving secretary a bear-hug, followed by a handshake. The next day, (business day) when they (the secretaries) met him, he was no different. He hugged them again. But they didn't hug each other. And that was a good omen for Granddad.

"When they sat for business, and each secretary introduced himself, he mentioned about Granddad's hug and handshake that strangely transformed his body and made him sleep deeply and soundly and he felt refreshed on awaking up the next day, and they wished that Granddad could offer them an explanation for the great and exhilarating feeling. The last secretary asked as to whether there was any secret regarding transforming others by hugs or handshakes. The nine others then said they would have asked the same question, and proceeded to ask Granddad the same question.

"'I would not be able to say it in words, but it is for religion and for political correctness' sake that the experience you had is the secret from a religion,' Granddad mentioned to them.

"Before the lunch break, Ella, Ziina and I went to meet them and hugged each of them calling them 'uncle'. We served them dinner. And when the conversions of their aircrafts were done and they had to leave at night, they opted to spend another night, in their own words, 'To understand understood issues of life'.

"The next day, as if they had met and planned it, they informed Granddad that they had informed their respective home countries of the need to understand the workings of the 'lepoid gas', any side effects, and why it was only available on Vota island. But their true intent was to have an understanding of what triggered their transformed bodies. Granddad could not tell them the reason or non-reason. Because when speaking to representatives of the people of the nations in the various countries, you must be politically correct in usage of language, as it was a universal crime and you could be arrested anyway and tried elsewhere.

"Then one of them, the one who was first to ask Granddad the secret behind their transformed bodies, said, 'When I travel through airports and the fingers of men rubbed against me or touched me, it was as if they had put something, no, an ill health into my body, or taken out the good health in me and put nothing there.'

"Granddad said nothing as a response. And one after the other, the other nine recounted similar experiences as the first. We should not be subject to the search regime like ordinary travellers, as we must not suffer ill-health or other negative consequences because of our responsibilities. And we pay much money just to get into a healthy shape to carry on our functions at the destination country.

"Hmm! If we count the cost of ill-health suffered by the hundreds of millions of our people, travellers because of those fingers rubbing or touching their bodies, we must not just appoint or employ every unemployed. But my proposal will amount to discrimination, if some cannot be recruited on the basis of their finger rubs or touches.

"Granddad then asked that each commission the three top university researchers to do a study. He offered to allow a thousand members of his family to be recruited as security men and women, but not for any monetary compensation, and as a control group. He also suggested that researchers should mount health-screening machines at a spot before security and another after security.

"We were told the researchers were wowed by Granddad's suggestion, wondering whether he was a researcher himself. Two million travellers were recruited for the first two-day experiments. Their health records were taken before security, followed by the searches of their bodies through rubs or touching by security men or women. And after that, the health records were extracted again.

"The Melon Elembele family's thousand members did searches on two hundred thousand travellers in the manner recommended by the protocol. The 1.8 million were handled by security men and women of the people of the nations. The results given to Granddad by the secretaries were as follows:

"1. Traveller; 2. Health status before security; 3. Security check; 4. Whom by, male or female; 5. People of the nations or Melon E family; 6. Post-security health status.

"You should note that in this study, women were allowed to search male travellers, but men were not allowed to search female travellers.

"The results of the Elembele family members were consistent with what those ten secretaries experienced and expressed. Actually, it was even better for the travellers the Elembele female members searched. And as regards the searches by male and female security members of the people of the nations, the post-security health status dipped below the pre-security health status. Again, their female security results, like the female Elembele security results, were better than their male counterparts though they dipped—"

"He-he-he! Will they recruit Elembele family members to provide security at all airports then?" Melon Jnr interrupted Anna to ask.

124

"Granddad only wanted to teach a lesson, and he has taught it. As in a politically correct environment, your words must be few. But studies must be conducted by researchers in top universities to effect changes," Anna explained.

"Eh, always? That would be expensive. And take away a chunk of their resources to effect every change or any change at any time," Melon Jnr expressed.

CHAPTER 33

The blood mark (the null symbol) in our passports

Jacksonville, FL, USA. November 15, 2017

"Granddad said concerning biometric passports that, 'You take it at your personal risk that if it has your death warrant embodied in it, instructing persons at a particular airport or country to arrest and murder you, you must travel always with angelic hosts from Mawu Sokpolisa to override the written edicts in it. For those who read must read what Mawu Sokpolisa has written about you, not what an earthling agent (who looks at your face and finds displeasure) has written,'" Anna said, and took many minutes thereafter to sip her 'cocoa-cafe' without any more word.

Unsettled thereby, Melon Jnr said, "Our weapons to defeat them at their game consist of words spoken to Mawu Sokpolisa to reveal his lightnings and thunders to confuse them. For who and what can stand those fearsome neutralizing weapons and defences? Before they take out one of us, Mawu Sokpolisa will take out a thousand of them with what they've fashioned out for our destruction."

Anna started weeping with bitterness of heart, and her tears were droplets of blood, and when Melon Jnr looked at the handkerchief she used to mop her tears, it had the appearance of blood clot balls the size of the circumference of one ten-cent coin. Melon Jnr therefore said, "The angelic hosts are crying through you, because Mawu Sokpolisa will strike at them and blood will flow in their land like rivers, swift-flowing, because they have plotted for many years against us or our family."

"Wow! That was a revelation to you and you spoke it as a prophet would. When Ziina told us, Granddad excluded that as we passed through many airport terminals in many countries, our biometric passports had had embossed in them the null symbol, a symbol that instructs the person in charge of scanning passports to alert all in security at destination or arrival airports to kill the passport holder with any weapon. And such a murderer would not be subject to any arrest or trial, because those who inserted the null symbol in their passports were deemed beings of other planets and therefore intruders on Earth causing discomfort and despair to those of the Earth – the people of the nations in the various countries of the world.

"She added that though the persons that scan the passports communicate the null symbol regarding us to them, they are so inconsistent that, a few seconds later, they countermand the earlier null symbol and mention the watching 'eye symbol' to show that we are watchers with that worldwide institution that took whatever decision needed as to what destruction occurs or occurred on Earth because he that they served liked and lived disorder. They live on blood flow in some countries, except their own island state and the numbered states that subscribe to its protection," Anna said.

"Twenty years since the carrying of biometric passports through multiple airports, but safe and will remain safe because under whom we subscribed our faith is Mawu Sokpolisa. Did you ever mention what Ziina told you and Ella to Granddad?" Melon Jnr asked.

"Yes. But he only said, 'When you have human-made arsenal to destroy Mawu Sokpolisa-protected vessels, they are impenetrable.' But the more I think of the thousands of persons of the people of the nations in the various countries of the world poised ready to kill us, but without our knowing till recently, the more I cried for them with weeping. And the hosts of angels wept through us because of their soon destruction, they, the people of the nations in the various countries of the world," Anna explained.

"The null symbol is always mistakenly read as the 'watching eye symbol' or multiplication symbol. And that was why none of us was ever killed. That was what Granddad mentioned one day mistakenly to me," Melon Jnr said.

CHAPTER 34

Daily invocations; the Granddad method

Jacksonville, FL, USA. November 15, 2017

"He woke me up at 5.00am. He was on his knees, no footwear on, and bowed his forehead to touch the floor. I also did. Then I heard words, 'Mawu Sokpolisa, enugake (Almighty God, it is yet another day), Medzeklonawo (I have knelt in your presence), Medetagonawo (I have bowed my forehead in reverence to you), Fafaneva (Let there be safety), Nutifafa neva (Let peace prevail), Xebiso (The lightning that questions the thunder), Mawu Sokpolisa enugake (Almighty God, it is another day), Medzeklonawo (I have knelt in your presence), Medetagonawo (I have bowed my forehead in reverence to you), Fafaneva (Let there be safety), Nutifafa neva (Let peace prevail).' And for a third time, the same words were repeated: 'Mawu Sokpolisa (Almighty God), Xebiso (The lightning that questions the thunder), Enugake (It is another day), Medzeklonawo (I have knelt in your presence), Medetagonawo (I have bowed my forehead in reverence), Fafaneva (Let there be safety), Nutifafa neva (Let peace prevail).' He sat up for a minute and then stood up on his feet. I did likewise. And I followed him to breakfast.

"Some thirty minutes later we were on our way to the first meeting, and our day ended, and after supper or dinner, I followed him again to what I would learn later as the prayer room.

"Granddad took off his shoes, went on his knees again as in the morning. And then his head bowed touching the floor. And he spoke words as follows: 'Mawu Sokpolisa, Xebiso zado

(Almighty God, the lightning that questions the thunder, it is night time), Medzeklonawo (I have knelt in your presence), Medetagonawo (I have bowed my forehead in reverence to you), Akpe nawo (Thanks), Fafa neva (Let there be safety), Nutifafa neva (Let peace prevail).

"There was a repetition a second time and a third time, and I echoed everything he did. A further one minute on his knees, and he stood up. And we went to the living room, where he chatted some hours of the night away with me and, at midnight, we went to our various rooms to sleep.

"The second day he woke me up. We did the morning prayers. At the day's end, the evening prayers. For the next five days, we didn't fail to do our twice-daily invocations and thanksgiving respectively.

"On the eighth day, Granddad thought I had overslept. But I also imagined that it could be a deliberate act. I got up and went to the prayer room and did my invocations as I learnt from him those first seven days. We met at breakfast. He didn't say anything or ask anything about invocations. I offered nothing as statement on it. We did our itineraries for the day. At close of day I went to the prayer room, and failed not to invoke and thanked Mawu Sokpolisa, Xebiso.

"On the night before we left Volvalu the next morning, Xebiso descended on the land of twenty million people, who had for many years before our visit performed human sacrifices of one man and one woman for each one million people every year, so we learnt, causing utter destruction of houses, animals and trees. Two houses were left of each million homes, possibly the houses of those sacrificial adult humans of each year. But none of the people died, but without a dwelling or residential properties, their head chief approached us as to what we could do to help. Granddad told them he was able to rebuild houses for them but they must serve and worship his god, Mawu Sokpolisa, and that Mawu Sokpolisa abhors human sacrifices. And that no god desires human sacrifices. And humans who wish to bring other humans under subjection, kill them, drink their blood and pretend to be doing it on behalf or for a god.

"He also explained that it was Mawu Sokpolisa who sent Xebiso, an aspect of Mawu Sokpolisa to cause the devastation of the land because of the human sacrifices. But he interrupted Granddad to say that he thought a god would not drink water or any drink but the blood of humans, and since the god made a man and a woman, they offered a pair every year as a sacrifice.

"'Well, the god who made the man and woman (Mawu Sokpolisa) was displeased with you because you did wrong in killing a man and woman, as that was not its intention when it made life to praise him with the words of their mouths, the beauty of their bodies, to smell the scent or aroma of Mawu Sokpolisa with their nostrils and offer praise.'

"He left us sullen, and didn't get back to Granddad as to whether Mawu Sokpolisa would be their god. A few weeks later, lightning scorched their bodies and the bowels of Earth opened and buried all of them. Then did we go back, when in a vision of the night it was revealed to me that there was bare land with only vegetation, but no people. I informed Granddad of the vision. He said it was the land of Volvalu. He sent me to verify, and it has become settlement for Melon Elembele family."

"Anna, you know that the type of people who dwell on any land determines the destiny or future of the land, its continued habitation or not. The people of Volvalu were no different from the people of the nations in the various countries of the world in what they did. But our dwelling among the people of the nations is what has not made Mawu Sokpolisa to send Xebiso to destroy them. We need a place or places of refuge when Mawu Sokpolisa strikes. And one such place is the land of Volvalu. And with our relocation, Mawu Sokpolisa will begin to destroy the people of the nations in the various countries of the world from their respective lands," Melon Jnr said.

"But we have other places of refuge. Mawu Sokpolisa is able to instruct Xebiso to distinguish between the people of the nations in the various countries of the world and Melon Elembele family members. It is just that it is a painstaking and patient work, as the angels of death move from house to house to execute judgment. I will tell you a scenario or two," Anna said.

"Whatever you have experienced in the past remains a 'teacher' to you to teach others, and the more graphic the better, because it teaches all the senses," Melon Jnr mentioned.

"When you see the rain fall in your neighbour's house, but not yours, then you know that those on Earth have no power to order what Mawu Sokpolisa has made as blessings for its invocators, and also weapons against their enemies be available to everyone. Have you seen the rain fall in our home but not in the neighbours' who are of the people of the nations?" Anna asked.

"Many, many times, but my memory can't remember all. Even the rays of the sun had shown in our home, while snow blizzards affected our immediate neighbour. The people of the nations in the neighbouring houses had attributed it to Granddad's witchcraft and worship of the sun god. But I knew it is Mawu Sokpolisa who controls and orders all the elements of nature to do its pleasure," Melon answered.

"Granddad and I had travelled to one country of the people of nations to inspect facilities. We rented two one-bedroom apartments. Strangely, the female block of apartments was separated by a five-mile-long grassless field. Maybe it was a park for an emergency settlement, should an earthquake occur? My apartment was on a second floor, hedged in by first-floor and third-floor apartments, in addition to what was opposite mine and also to my north and south. Granddad's was in a similar position in the male-occupied block of apartments.

"We don't travel anywhere without doing our invocations and divining, or asking whether to go or not of Mawu Sokpolisa. When a yes answer was received, we were certain of absolute protection. And also, didn't forget to invoke that name while in the destination place. Two times we would do that every day, as Granddad taught you. The third night in our apartments, lightning struck in select apartments, even those of our closest neighbours, but we slept and woke up the next day sound, and the fire service personnel wondered how lightning could strike and set fire to neighbours' apartments, below, above, opposite, to the north and south, but not ours.

"We were therefore deported that same morning, and all our facilities were seized and closed in that country. One day, with you in the saddle, it may become a barren and bare land for us to go in, put up buildings for the Melon Elembele family, changing the land's destiny. I think I don't want to mention any more examples. Look for opportunities to experience these events and be fulfilled, so that you can declare that Mawu Sokpolisa, the Xebiso, is like no other god."

CHAPTER 35

The 299 dogs assigned to guard us

Jacksonville, FL, USA. November 16, 2017

"Melon Jnr, I didn't tell you all that happened when we were deported. We had to go through a transit country. And Ella and Ziina and Vanguard were to come over to the country we were deported from and therefore Granddad asked them to meet us in the transit country. Their flight landed a few minutes before our flight. And they were in the waiting area when we also entered to wait for two and a half hours and then fly out on the next leg. Granddad was telling them about our deportation reason when two guards entered and asked to inspect our passports. Granddad took my mine and added his to it and handed them to one of the two guards. He flipped through quickly and didn't notice anything that needed further scrutiny or questions and passed them to his colleague. He pored over each page and possibly saw the word 'DEPORTED' in capital letters in both passports.

"He went away with the passports and returned thirty minutes later with a woman who most likely was higher in status. She asked the two of us to follow them to another location not far away from the transit waiting area. When we stepped out with the three of them, she mentioned that the country we were deported from had informed them when they checked the reason for our deportation that we were dangerous persons, not fit to be among the people of the nations. She mentioned that when she pressed for more information, she was told, and that she was quoting the officer who spoke to her, 'The elderly man and the young woman

134

brought strange lightning that set fire to all apartments and persons within those apartments, except their two apartments located at the male and female sections respectively. We saw the unbelievable but believable ashes and bones of properties and the dead, but they were untouched personally in any way, nor the apartment each occupied, and we realized they were threat to property and human security and deported them'.

"'Please, you are dangerous and cannot be part of human beings in any building. We will keep you with the dogs, and when your flight is ready we will escort you to your aircraft,' the female officer said.

"We were taken to a holding place for dogs as we couldn't offer any explanation or defence for what happened in the first country to exculpate ourselves. Melon, how would you explain an act of Xebiso to a people who knew nothing about Mawu Sokpolisa?

"And not even an hour and a half later, all the dogs were dead, to our shock. I think they saw the dying dogs through their CCTV cameras, for the woman, the two men, and fifty other guards rushed to the holding area and pointed at us to follow them. We did, and we were put on our aircraft. Granddad drew their attention to Ella, Ziina and Vanguard as part of us, and they hurried and brought them and put them on the flight. And the female officer spoke saying, 'We are safer with you on board your aircraft till your departure.' 'Thank you,' we all answered.

"We were quiet through our return journey of seven hours, except for meal or snack times, we all pondering about the mysteries associated with the Melon Elembele family. I cannot explain why Ella and Ziina were also quiet like me and Granddad. But I know that when your Granddad is quiet, you must also be quiet.

"I remember the 299 dogs with sorrow, but when it was the judgment and punishment of Mawu Sokpolisa through Xebiso, your remembrance must be fleeting. And it was. Will you kneel on the floor, bow your forehead to touch the floor on my behalf . . ."

Anna didn't complete her statement as Melon Jnr knelt and echoed other acts in reverence to Mawu Sokpolisa.

CHAPTER 36

The beauty of the mind's clock of time and the clock of time

Jacksonville, FL, USA. November 17, 2017

"When your mind's clock is faster than the clock of time, you have rest for body and sicknesses, and ill health will not come near you. He or she that operates the mind's clock lives a heavenly existence on Earth," Anna mentioned to Melon one morning after their deportation from one country and their restraint in a second country.

"You talk about serenity, that state derived from the mind's clock that can only be found by a few millions. And fewer millions find it in their lives daily. Granddad maybe, is one such example. But I discount myself from it. When your mind's clock runs at twice the clock's time, it is because your mind is at rest, nothing fills the mind to make it equal to the time clock," Melon explained.

"I learnt years ago through Granddad about the mind's clock. We had, after a stressful two weeks, landed in a country of the people of the nations, but it had many Melon Elembele family members doing or rendering services in addition to the operations of the big or heavy industries, and/or malls. Tiska was involved in providing massage services. We booked for a one-hour massage from her, glad that Wento, a massager of the people of the nations, had declined to massage him, and I, when she saw our cell phone numbers on hers. 'Honey,' Tiska had said to Granddad when we arrived in her parlour. She directed him to a room to change, and he did. And she massaged him for one hour exactly, because he saw the start time and end time on the clock of time. But his mind's clock registered thirty minutes. How could that be? he protested to Tiska.

"'It is when there is no distraction in your mind. For when you are looking at the clock of time, then views, events or things are twice faster, and you achieve twice the result, and the clock of time is meaningless to you as a measure of time,' Tiska explained.

"'Oh! Tiska, you mean to say that when the clock of time no more means anything to you, and is not used as a measure but the mind's time, you achieve twice for the clock of time measure? And there is therefore not fretting when you measure your results?' Granddad said. And she assured him again as follows: 'A state of mind, where and when you begin to see things or achieve results twice within the clock of time, means you have developed the mind's clock to compete with the clock of time for twice the results. And that time is called serenity.'

"I also did the massage and found that I had the mind's clock of time, but not the clock of time. With time, each member developed the mind's clock of time. No irritation arises if you develop the mind's clock of time. And since those early years of the Melon Elembele family, we have adopted and used the mind's clock of time rather than the clock of time," Anna stated.

CHAPTER 37

Deaths of ten princes and ten princesses as gratitude

Jacksonville, FL, USA. November 16, 2017

"Five princes and five princesses have died. A prince on turning forty years of age died. And while a princess, on turning twenty-eight years, died–" Anna was saying.

"What an introduction, Anna! Is it a lecture to students to capture their attention from all those tech gadgets that don't allow for our five senses to be used most times, but only one sense of those senses?" Melon interrupted Anna to ask.

"How I wish they were mine. I would have reduced it into written form and thereby be the copyright holder. They are Granddad's. The introduction to a story he told our parents and who also told us," Anna answered.

"With such an intro, I am yearning to listen and hear it all with the patience of a woman telling a story to the boyfriend, but the impatience of a husband whose mind is on her beautiful body and what it would do to him when she leant against him," Melon Jnr said.

"I hope that is not a cue for me to take. And if it is, it will have to wait till the end of time, which could be thousands of years or a moment.

"Granddad had operations – malls, industries, farms, hospitals, etc – in a number of kingdoms of the people of the nations. And Granddad was worried that with no successor to the kings or queens, if all the princes and princesses died without an heir or heiress, and a servant seized or usurped the throne, his properties could be in jeopardy. He didn't hesitate to pay visits to the neighbouring kingdoms whose kings sought for his counsel.

"I will speak as if I were Granddad and travelled to the three kingdoms one after the other: When I arrived at night in the month of August in Lepopotin Kingdom, I was met at their international airport and pulled in a horse-drawn carriage – traditional modernity had not touched the kingdom.

"The palace was in darkness; not a single light was on because as I later learned, they were into the second month of mourning for the last dead prince and princess who could only be buried after 120 days and nights of mourning. The king and queen had their heads bowed down in accordance with their custom, and when my presence was announced to them, a fleeting smile came on their faces, again in accordance with custom for a visitor to the royal courts, even during bereavement must be smiled at as a sign of warm welcome. And when informed of the death, the visitor would also bow his head down unsmiling, I learnt, till another visitor enters, when the mourners again put on a fleeting smile.

"The king, when I was given a stool to sit on and sat, spoke not looking into my eyes: 'Metutu Family was not the original royal family. Metutu, our forebear, was a loyal servant in the king's palace and the courtyards. The king didn't go on a visit to any part of the kingdom, unless he was advised by Metutu to do so. And Metutu also controlled the sleeping and waking up times of the king, and arranged for when the queen must visit the king's bedroom to spend the night. And these were few and far between. The king, did not know that Metutu only arranged the queen's visit to his bedroom when her ovulation period was three days past. The king therefore didn't ever make the wife pregnant for a prince or princess to be born to succeed the king.

"'The king died one night without a successor, and Metutu arranged for the queen to pay a visit to the king in his bedroom. This time, he specified a time of 10 o'clock in the night. The queen was in her ovulation period to the knowledge of Metutu.

Metutu went ahead of the queen to the king's bedroom, removed the king's corpse to another room, and lay on the royal bed expectantly waiting for the queen (that was what our forebear told us). She entered and laid by the king, so she thought. Her body, when it touched the 'king', felt sensitivities that she had not felt ever in her marriage. And she yielded to the 'king' in all that he wanted. And before she left the king's bedroom at dawn, she expressed her gratitude, and added that she felt that she would be pregnant because of the unusual feelings.

"'At her words, Metutu lowered the clothing covering his face partially to kiss her (that was what he told us), and he was in the act of still kissing her, when his face covering fell completely and the queen screamed.

"'Other courtiers (counsellors), two of them, thinking something was amiss, rushed into the king's bedroom and found Metutu and the queen. They would have put a spear through his heart, but he told them that it was the king who arranged for him to sleep with the queen. The counsellors then told him that he and the king were wrong, and the king must die and he, Metutu, must pacify the gods. And so, our ancestor Metutu, because his conscience was heavy for being caught doing wrong, went in a hurry with them and the queen to the next room that held the effigy of the gods.

"'He swore to the gods that if he became king, he would, from a certain period, annually give the best gifts to the gods and goddesses as his gratitude. He became king, but didn't live long enough to see the birth of his only son with the queen. And because the queen was pregnant with a child, she became a caretaker king till her child should be of age to ascend the throne. I am that son. I became of age and ascended the throne. I gave birth to six princes and six princesses. There is a twelve-year gap between each prince and a princess. And so far, five princes have died on reaching the age of forty. And five princesses died, each when she reached the age of twenty-eight.

"'With one of each left, I might die without a rightful heir, but a type of Metutu. You have travelled the world to countries of the people of the nations, and with your family people. Maybe there is a god you know, or a medicine that can be used, to preserve the last prince and last princess,' King Metutu the Second said.

"'I know not of any medicine that can help your situation. But I know of a god, Mawu Sokpolisa that can rescue you and the prince and princess from soon death,' Granddad said.

"Why did he swear such an oath to gods and goddesses without specifying what he meant by best gifts? In my many years on Earth and serving Mawu Sokpolisa, no human, man or woman swears an oath to a god or goddesses to give them the best seasonally when they help you. What you have is theirs, or Mawu Sokpolisa's. He (your ancestor) is only a steward of what belongs to gods or goddesses or Mawu Sokpolisa. Had he not ever heard of a man (a god) who came to Earth, and one day sent his disciples to bring a colt or a donkey from another village to him, and explained to them that if anyone should ask them why they were taking the leash off, they must tell him that the Lord needed it, and he would allow them to take it?

"And so, nothing is ever ours but for gods, goddesses and Mawu Sokpolisa. And if you must make or swear an oath to a god, specify exactly what you will give and at what time periods. With Mawu Sokpolisa, my words (even of my family members) daily in the morning or evening are: 'Mawu Sokpolisa, enugake, (Almighty God, it is yet another day), Medzeklonawo (I have knelt in your presence), Medetagonawo (I have bowed my forehead in reverence to you), Fafaneva (Let there be safety), Nutifafa neva (Let peace prevail), Xebiso (The lightning that questions the thunder), Mawu Sokpolisa, enugake (Almighty God, it is another day), Medzeklonawo (I have knelt in your presence), Medetagonawo (I have bowed my forehead in reverence to you), Fafaneva (Let there be safety), Nutifafa neva (Let peace prevail).' And for a third time, the same words were repeated: 'Mawu Sokpolisa (Almighty God), Xebiso (The lightning that questions the thunder), Enugake (It is another day), Medzeklonawo (I have knelt in your presence), Medetagonawo (I have bowed my forehead in reverence), Fafaneva (Let there be safety), Nutifafa neva (Let peace prevail), Mawu Sokpolisa.'

"I could petition Mawu Sokpolisa for you. Because, Mawu Sokpolisa overrides the dictates of other gods and goddesses, or gets them to cancel them and not hold it against your ancestor or his successor. The only cost to you is a prayer room, your feet off from the kingly sandals, your knees bowed to the floor or ground, your forehead touching the ground or floor in obeisance, and the invocations, I have mentioned.

"'How can I go on my knees and also my forehead bowed and touching the floor in obeisance? I will be removed. No king does that,' King Metutu the Second said. 'Kings are not obliged to follow what subjects or other mortals did or do,' Granddad replied. 'You sought my advice and I have given it to you. The throne did not belong to your family to start with. And if you die, and the last prince and last princess die, it might go to another royal family line or another usurper.' 'I will do what you've advised tomorrow morning. Good night Mr. Melon Elembele,' King Metutu the Second said.

"The next morning, King Metutu the Second was found dead, and also the last prince and the last princess, Granddad informed us."

"Their gods or goddesses, didn't want to be countermanded by Mawu Sokpolisa, and they took their lives that night a few hours before the morning," Melon Jnr said.

"If it is a matter involving gods, goddesses and Mawu Sokpolisa, the instant moment is your moment to act and not a deferred time of your choosing," Anna explained.

CHAPTER 38

What death and why?

Jacksonville, FL, USA. November 19, 2017.

““The restaurant sat not more than seven diners at any one time, but many more would have eaten their food, most of it as takeout. And each day, before its doors were closed at 11:30pm, it will have served two thousand different meals, most of it to the people of the nations.

“Granddad and I had eaten there in the past. Our flight had arrived rather late at night, beyond the arrival time of 6 o’clock in the evening, local time. We opted for something sizzling hot and they gave us just that. Taste was pleased and we looked forward for another time. I don’t know why each of the five senses only think of itself when it is not independent of the other four and also other body parts. If the sense of taste were living on its own, it would have stayed on in that country with the restaurant. But that not being the case, Anna, without taste buds, would have been looked at as having sold the taste buds to those who were and are more active at night, forgetting friends and biological family, and having friends and family as those who roam and work at night, not what normal work entails but drinking the blood of others or selling their sperm to those who don’t need it for fertilization of an egg, but to ‘fertilize’ money to birth many folds.

“Here was I alone on this second trip, and my tongue reminded me of that previous trip, and so, without a shower, I drove there. A ten-year-old boy took my order of only fried things. Ten minutes later, I was walking to the car and I smelt the scent of urine, but the air I think blew it away. But the scent was unmistakable when I slammed the car door shut with the takeout food in it. Was there a leak into my panties without my knowing, and more so when it was not more than thirty minutes ago when I had taken my shower and the urine voluntarily came out?

"Hmm! Maybe the nostrils wanted to deny the taste buds what it had desired for over a year and three months. Could the senses be envious of each other, like it was happening to the people of the nations in the various countries of the world? And if such were to happen, who loses? Not the senses, but Anna.

"I stopped in front of a grocery shop to pick a few breakfast items and took the takeaway food in with me. Too many people of the nations looked in my direction at the till where I was paying, but the till attendant didn't give any indication that anything was amiss. When I stepped out of the grocery store doors, hey, a stronger urine scent hit my nostrils. I reasoned that the sewage scent was coming out of sewers in the ground, which the ground refused to take because it didn't have sufficient air bubbles within its soil, and had transferred the scent to the air for a good neighbourly assistance, hence the stronger scent.

"I invoked Mawu Sokpolisa to protect me from bacteria or germs when I ate the food. For when hungry, the decision of the nostrils out of envy can be your undoing if you should throw away the food into the trash bag. It also likes sweet and pleasant aromas, but the best aromas are not the tastier tastes to the taste buds. And so, I ate a portion for supper. I smelt what I had left over and put it in the fridge overnight. The next morning, there was no urine scent and so I warmed it for brunch.

"I returned to the restaurant at evening time for another treat, but it was closed with a notice outside its doors saying that the owners had lost their ten-year-old son. He died in his sleep. When I went and sat in my car, I recalled that I felt in my spirit in the restaurant the night before that the boy had done something wrong. But the mum only smiled at him, and he smiled back, as the people of the nations were wont to do when someone does a wrong and they cover it with two smiles of deceit to humans but not to a god or Mawu Sokpolisa. I felt certain that he had been killed by a god. And I hoped that the parents and other relations would know so that next time when someone did a wrong they would not cover it with a smile, but reproof and correction, for humans may not see, but their gods see and exact punishment.

"A week later, I went again to that restaurant. And when they saw me, they waved at me to step away. I asked, 'No food?' The mother said, 'No food for you,' meaning I, Anna. I was about to drive away when the father banged his hand on my side door. I instructed the glass windows to roll down and they did. 'I am sincerely sorry. I didn't see him do what he did to your order. But the mum did. He mentioned what he did when he realized that the smiles of his and those of the mother didn't cover the wrong, and you not seeing it and complaining. But someone saw and took action, hence his death. Maybe she also would have added something to your meal today and would also be seen by whatever saw the son (no, our son) and killed him, and would have killed her also. And I would not have seen her and would have lost two to death in eight or nine days. Please, you have a better protection, not of the courts of law, or fortresses, but a securer (divine) protection, for I saw that it works backwards and forwards.' And so, I went away and didn't eat that night, not of fear but to honour Mawu Sokpolisa who took away the hunger pangs and taste desires of my taste buds," Anna explained.

"Eh! It was good they knew about the death and why. If you don't know, you will slowly die off, one by one, until no one is left for you," Melon Jnr mentioned.

While Anna said, "I will talk about one more tragic event, about a person of the people of the nations on that trip. Mawu Sokpolisa's protection transcends everything we did or do. For two consecutive Sundays, I went to a particular church. I put money in the offering envelope without writing my name and amount because there was no pen to do that. Weeks later, I was told the elderly usher who took the envelopes without names on as empty to throw away instead of their reuse, knew money was in the them. He noticed visitors to the church and ensured that when they were putting money in the envelopes he saw it and took advantage to line his own pockets (as the church practiced online giving, that he detested). And although other ushers tried to help him to open the envelopes, whether written on or not, he told them off, with the explanation that those envelopes should not be checked or opened or reused, for it is witches who don't write their names or amounts on envelopes, but puts the empty envelope in the offering basket to take money away for them, the witches. The other ushers bought into the explanation because of his age and his fifty-plus service as an usher.

"Well, like I felt in the restaurant that something was amiss, the second Sunday, it was more pronounced that I would not receive blessings because my offering was going elsewhere. The third Sunday he was not at church. I arrived in church with a younger man. Awhile later, the pastor came over with an usher and asked that we go to the church office. We did. And he said the elderly usher blamed me for killing him with thunder and lightning when he was slowly dying. 'Why would I do that?' I screamed, and also said, 'I am only on a visit to your country and therefore church.' The pastor then said, 'He took your offerings from the envelopes, that could only be the explanation.' And he then mentioned to me the earlier statements that I said to you. 'My apologies, sincerely,' the pastor said.

"They hosted me a lunch after church and I assured them that any time I was in their country alone, or with others, we would have fellowship with them. Two years on, with six different visits, two with Granddad, Ella and Ziina, the pastor and church members became members of the Melon Elembele family. That was how Granddad, by not setting up a church (except churches in our homes for two times daily worship), had the first temple and other family temples came into being, dedicated to Mawu Sokpolisa," Anna related to the hubby.

"Oh! Is that why there are numbered temples tagged to Mawu Sokpolisa's name?" Melon asked.

"Yes, for remembrance of historical facts easily, and their knowing what death is and why," Anna mentioned.

CHAPTER 39

When some family members neglected

Jacksonville, FL, USA. November 20, 2017.

"The Thursday, that Thursday, must be remembered in our family because it was the day of our awakening. We almost failed the task Granddad gave us, and almost destroyed what he had built and assigned to us to build on," Anna said.

"Oh, I thought, and I am inclined to believe, that bad patches in any people's or family's life overcome must be forgotten and not ever remembered, especially when it ended well," Melon Jnr responded.

"Not in a Melon Elembele family. It must be recounted at yearly intervals and a 'festival of heads and knees bowed for one continuous hour' (while repeating the words: 'Mawu Sokpolisa (God Almighty), Woekonye Mawu (You only are God), Medzeklonawo (I have knelt in your presence), Medetagonawo (I have bowed my forehead in reverence to you), Ngoyiyi nevadzi (There must be development),' intermittently held in honour of Mawu Sokpolisa, the Xebiso. Were it not that you turned our failure and destruction into success, the people of the nations would have mocked us, saying they knew that it was only a matter of time when our failure and destruction would also come. For to them, there is no god who ensures or sees to the goodness of its people throughout all generations, but makes failure of some generations so that it (the god) can be seen as the only non-failure ever. But Mawu Sokpolisa is unlike their gods. Mawu Sokpolisa will awaken you to your failures, or failings with lightning and thunders, and when those are understood by you and you change course to continue on the ancient but true paths, your success continues like its names," Anna said.

"Then may I recount the events of that Thursday as a rehearsal in preparation for the anniversary, when it will be my lot with the many millions of the family members to thank Mawu Sokpolisa in the manner you mentioned?" Melon Jnr asked.

"I will defer to you as much as it will be your obligation to lead the set of eleven to fifteen-year-olds, and the set of sixteen to twenty-year-olds, the Melonites and Melontities respectively, in the festival," Anna explained.

Melon Elembele Jnr went on his knees and would have started recounting the events, but Anna advised that that was not the way to go. The events must be recounted standing as the festival begins with the kneeling and the bowed head for one hour while mentioning the words mentioned.

"A woman or wife who reminds a man or husband of the good way of doing things but rebukes him not, plays her complementary role for mutual success. Thanks, Anna.

"That Thursday was the third Thursday when the named age groups had failed to go into the woods or forests to walk through them, admiring and chatting, and also hearing the instructions of Mawu Sokpolisa for working on ideas creation. They chose to stay indoors to play with technology gadgets, unbeknownst to me and Anna, and our failings began from that first Thursday because no fresh ideas came to the various groups as they heard no instructions from Mawu Sokpolisa in the woods. And then the second Thursday. And the third also. But that Thursday, the sky darkened before the sun set and Mawu Sokpolisa, the Xebiso, became thunders that filled the sky with lightning flashes that descended on Earth in majesty, but fearsome, kicked out the technology gadgets from their hands. And terrified that their end had come, the millions of them across various locations, that frantic were their voices on the 'reacher' device linked to Anna and me. And so, Anna and I asked, 'Did you go into the woods to walk among other activities?' And they said no, and that was the

149

third time in succession they decided not to go but play with technology devices.

"'It is Mawu Sokpolisa you have wronged by not walking through the woods every Thursday according to its statutes. You have received its warnings to continue in its statutes. We will ensure you do that because there are great rewards.' And we heard them on the interlinked 'reacher' communication lines: 'We had no rewards in terms of instructions and therefore ideas the past three Thursdays,' each said. 'We are better off with Mawu Sokpolisa, who is better than all technology. A walk, therefore, every Thursday through the woods,' they promised.

"But again, unbeknownst to us, they had often not risen at dawn to walk outside their sleeping places to have the dew of the dawn fall on them, and didn't do the daily invocations as Granddad would have wanted. Many therefore complained of ill health most days, an unusual occurrence in a Melon Elembele family. And we therefore tapped the 'reacher' to find out if what had been put on their hearts with regard to going out at dawn for the dew were so. And our fears were confirmed. And when they resorted to going out every day for the dew of the dawn, no more did any complain of ill health any day.

"And Mawu Sokpolisa, we want to do your will always, but being human with limitations, reveal your limitless knowledge to us. Then, with those words placed on my heart, I held the rehearsal, but I realised that the two age groups did not carry out a third obligation on three Sundays of walking barefooted three miles each on green lawns designed by Granddad for the purpose. And as a person walks and swears to Mawu Sokpolisa that he or she was walking on firm ground because Mawu Sokpolisa made it so, he or she would remain above the grass not ever below it.

"And when I finished recounting, Anna assured me that we were so dear to Mawu Sokpolisa because of our calling out the name, and obedience would keep us as strong and powerful as Mawu Sokpolisa. And that made me remember the events Anna mentioned about what deaths and why. And, after it all, the one hour on my knees with forehead bowed and reciting words also came to an end, satisfied of the surpassing greatness in the future," Melon Jnr said.

CHAPTER 40

What will make a woman have more than the benefactor?

Jacksonville, FL, USA. November 20, 2017

"She was not a wife to him. Neither a girlfriend who with time could become a lover or loved for the things that are only within the hearts," Anna said.

"Hmm! There was no potential around her (a magic) that could speak for her to change her status to a closer type of relationship, a member of the family!" Melon Jnr said.

"As if you knew. But Granddad had initially thought that if she showed that she had what it took by not behaving like a young woman of the people of the nations, she could work in one of the malls. And he actually started her off with recording articles that were taken off sales stock and put away to be donated. Within the first six months, when Granddad asked that she should render accounts, she got angry at him, and said she knew she would have to render accounts at year-end, not earlier. He kept quiet. The year-end came, and no accounts were rendered. Two years on, she spoke about no account. So, while she came and ate with us, the items to have kept records on were put under another woman's care.

"And not a day passes when she does not try to explain further whatever she had previously said. In many cases, when she thought the explanations would belie the earlier statement she spoke, she would give an excuse to go to the loo or washroom, and when she came back would either say she was unwell or go out to visit a family that lost a member weeks ago but which she forgot and had remembered. With that, she clothed herself with a mournful look. You would feel sympathetic towards her if you were to be present.

"And for at least three days, our meal times were without her. And Granddad would then send to find out whether she was well, as Granddad had explained that those whom they provided for fortunately know that those who provided for them owe a duty to provide for them who don't have, and if not done would annoy Mawu Sokpolisa. And she, as one of the have-nots before Mawu Sokpolisa, was owed a duty that we couldn't provide grudgingly but with a cheerful heart, otherwise Mawu Sokpolisa's judgment could descend on us. But they think wrongly that they don't have a corresponding obligation to act right.

"We were not at home when she came one day, took some money from the cashier and left a note for Granddad. Granddad was surprised that she left a note, and had hoped that she was changing, and the first step would lead to other good steps.

"Humans express hope, but only gods know the intents of the mind and of the heart of another human. With the money, she travelled to another country (we were told later) to meet a sorcerer who had assured her that if she brought money from a wealthy man's house, he could give her words to chant, and forever the wealthy man would give whatever he owns to her. But she had heard the words of the sorcerer wrongly, so the sorcerer explained when she returned and chanted the words and nothing ever was given to her by Granddad or any member of our family. She went back and the sorcerer told her that the money must come directly from the hands of Granddad, and not another.

"My husband, have you ever been to a sorcerer or read books written on them? When you give them money and they give you a charm or enchantment, they pre-emptively prepare the next reason why the charm or enchantment failed. And that way the charm or enchantment will not cease to feed them, for blessings come on the work of your hands or whatever body part you use;

but she didn't understand the ways of sorcerers that you will be their blessings for all time.

"She went to borrow money for needs and gave it to the sorcerer and, when the money lender was on her sleeves, she came to plead to be helped. Granddad gave her the money, plus two times the amount for her upkeep and she no more ate in our home.

"Hmm! Humans, when they unexpectedly have more in their pocket or bank accounts, think of how to multiply it but not how to work at earning more. And in seeking to do that, they lose it all. Money, well-deserved wealth, can only be added to but not multiplied. She was one such who will seek multiplication. She went back, and her smiles alone made the sorcerer suspect that she had come by good fortune. And whereupon, the sorcerer said, 'It was a matter of delayed working of the charm or enchantment. Has he not given you more than you needed and asked for? Before you entered, I knew the glow of happiness had clothed you. And when I also bask in that glow at night, my spirit will go with you to speak to his spirit for a continuous flow as I have mentioned to you.'

"Without hesitation, she gave all to him, except enough for food and transport back. She deceived Granddad in the name of a money lender chasing her, but a deceiver is many times more readily deceived, for deceit when multiplied, takes away your sense of reasoning and makes you see castles and wealth with only the eye. 'How did I become aware of these things?' her mother mentioned to us on her deathbed.

"After this second failure, she sought for five young men to kill us on a trip to a particular country of the people of the nations that we frequently visited. And she had planned that when in that country, they would waylay us on our way to the hotel, kill us, and with the key to our home go along with her to our home for whatever treasure she can find. And she therefore persistently asked as to when we would go visit, and when we informed her of three-day visit, and the dates, she informed the five men. But we visited but returned the same day. That was not as we had planned. But Mawu Sokpolisa commanded us to leave.

"The five men, having wasted what little they had, and not having achieved their aim, stabbed her in anger, and for many days she laid on her deathbed. And this was how she lost her life.

"Anyone who fed you once, or has ever provided you with any of this Earth's goods sacrificed for you, became a ransom. And you owe a like duty whether you know or not to be a ransom for the giver. And she became a ransom for us," Anna explained.

"Eh! What will make a woman and even men have more than their benefactors?" Melon Jnr asked.

"The answer lies in the events I have related. But to others, as much as humans live on Earth and are subject to Mawu Sokpolisa's rules, whether an adherent or not, nothing and nothing but death," Anna explained.

And Melon, wishing to have the last word, said, "Melon Elembele and his family members have many ransoms . . ."

CHAPTER 41

What is in your past? And will your past undo your future?

Jacksonville, FL, USA. November 21, 2017

"We were gathered for the family's first convention of granddaughters and grandsons. We ate, we danced to songs and beating of drums from all corners of the world. But not like the people of the nations of the world. There was no drunkenness, no smoking of any of the known things that teenagers of the people of the nations smoke. When we entered the night-time hours, no orgies occurred. At the stroke of midnight, we all retired to our individual rooms. And at breakfast the next day, Granddad spoke saying, 'When I was a teen, my mother and father, Mr and Mrs Yearning Elembele, informed me that I should not let my past write my future. And that they had allowed their past to write their future. And the only thing they as a couple ever agreed on was that your past can write your future. But they didn't explain how.

"And I set out to find out how. I spoke to my parents again as to how they came to the conclusion that the past could write a person's future. But they said they were told and they were only passing on that knowledge to me. I therefore spoke to more than a thousand other couples as to whether the past wrote a person's future. Their answer was yes. And as to an explanation, only twenty of them didn't say it was the trick of gods, their gods and goddesses, to make sure that those who lived on Earth (human beings) didn't live a different life from them and thereby know a different god (Mawu Sokpolisa) who would widen their minds to see more than Earth as the world, and aspire to be part of or be in that bigger world.

"And not desiring my future to be ruled by my past, I travelled far and wide, but still didn't get answer. I then began a search to find out whether other animals or birds looked down only at the ground and therefore Earth and would honour the Earth as god. In the small village and later a town we lived in, I never saw any animal or bird, (not even on the travels I took) soar into the skies looking upwards in search of another world and its god. But then my eyes fell on some beetles who'd burrowed into the ground (earth) under my feet building ten storeys many feet above the ground. The beetles made an opening to what they had built and so I entered. It was dark, but there were glittering lights pointing to a deep hole made by the beetles in the ground to be able to create the many-storied buildings above ground. I felt that if the beetles could burrow deep into the ground, then they could teach knowledge about a god or being that taught them that they could live above ground at certain times, and at other times in the storied homes. Consequently, their past didn't rule their future.

"I went back, looking into the skies to find what looked upwards. Not three months later, I saw a formation of eagles moving from east to west, looking further and further upwards. I moved in the direction they took. And I met a man in the woods next to a high mountain. He smiled at me and I smiled back. The language that speaks peace, warmth and love. He pointed at the eagles atop the mountain peak, plucking their feathers. I looked, and felt sad that they were losing their feathers and therefore with no feathers there would be no ability to fly again. And as if the man knew what was on my mind, he made a sign to indicate that they would fly again. I felt he must be more knowledgeable than my parents and the couples I spoke to in the past.

"'You are seeking for understanding as to why in the world of humans on Earth, the past rules their future. Because you don't want the past to rule your future,' he said. 'I don't,' I said to him. Then he leaned against a slope and asked me to also lean. I did.

Then he said, 'There was a god on Earth (the ground) before human beings were brought to the Earth as pilgrims so that in the future they could go to another place better than Earth. But that god didn't want to remain alone on Earth forever, and he had one peculiar knowledge that when your future is or was ruled by the past, you will not be able to move on to that other place.

"'And so the god (Damri) thought of what he could do so that humans' future would be ruled by their past. You may not know, but gods, like humans, have been endowed with brains, and whoever reasons hard enough will have what he desires to help achieve a purpose, Damri reasoned. Excited that when he got a human being to do the wrong thing, the human being would have to ask for his pardon and be forgiven, he told human beings that if they wronged each other, they could ask for pardon and be forgiven. But Damri didn't tell them that once they had done a wrong and been forgiven, if another person did a similar wrong to them, they must forgive also. He hardened their hearts not to forgive. And as a result, the earlier forgiveness granted became revoked and the wrong restored. And with many wrongs against each other, none would be able to move to the next place after Earth. Human beings forgot that it was Damri who made the past rule the future, and only told them that the past would rule their future. But that statement is a deceit by Damri passed on. The past actually ruins your future,' The man said.

"'Please, then is it possible for the past to not rule or ruin your future?' I asked. 'If and when you do a wrong, and you are pardoned, you must also pardon others wrongs against you and, more importantly, not even mention it. Have you read of that servant who had his debts forgiven by his master but held another servant and didn't forgive that servant's debts? The earlier debt forgiveness was revoked, and his indebtedness restored, and he was put in prison till he paid all. You must know that a prisoner cannot pay debts because he is in prison. And a prisoner doesn't qualify for the other place. So, unless you confess and be forgiven, your past will judge you,' the man answered me again and asked,

'Are you in condemnation of anyone who has done a similar thing? He that is without sin should cast the first stone.'

"The world from an early age ensnares you to sin and, because of that sin, you cannot ever condemn another, because once you do that your sin rises and is restored against you, and you also must be stoned, that the spirit would eventually manifest in the physical.

"Note that the servant who sinned against his master and his master forgave him, because he didn't forgive another who owed him less than he owed his master, the master revoked the forgiveness and threw him into jail till he had paid all. And so it is that Damri holds it against you so that you can never cast a stone. 'And so, grandchildren, I am going to build a Melon Elembele family, where the past must not rule or ruin anyone,' Granddad Melon concluded.

"We felt contented that not knowing what he would speak about at breakfast that morning we did no wrongs the previous night, because Granddad's good spirit lived in us not to do wrong. In the Melon Elembele family, we are not ruled by a past to rule our future, because Mawu Sokpolisa protects us from the snare of Damri," Anna concluded, and hugged the husband while stating, "You came into a good family to move onto that other place, but not the people of the nations in the various countries of the world."

CHAPTER 42

Granddad's modern-time redemption efforts

Jacksonville, FL, USA. November 21, 2017

"They were generally young, pretty and attractive women. They knew only the countries they hailed from as the world. But they told them of another country and another world. They showed them photos and videos of that new country. All was glamour, splendour, glitz, food joints and well-fed men and women walking serenely on paved roads with potted plants. The cars being driven on the six-lane roads in both directions were innumerable, with none carrying two persons. There were no contrasting images of the violence, murders, rapes, stench-filled streets, unlighted and unfinished huts along lanes with a few unfed girls wriggling their waists per chance a man with two meals for that day would offer her one meal in return for a kind act from her body, and in that way her family of five would be given a meal and not another day go without food," Anna said after dinner, when the husband asked her what memory of Granddad they could retire to bed with.

"Do I try to guess what you will be talking about tonight in his memory?" Melon Jnr asked.

"No guessing in a marital relationship that gives you all facts and figures and conceals nothing as private. I will tell you all, more than you have time for this evening if you want a wife's body to curl around yours," Anna said.

"No comment, but so that the story will end early, let other things unspoken begin," Melon Jnr responded.

"And so, in search of a new country and a new world that their eyes saw (the imaginations of photographers or videographers), their feet followed. They were in millions. And they (their employers) distributed them in many countries of the people of the nations of world. But in the new country and the new world, the unreality of those photos and videos they saw glared at them. But none could return to their home countries, because their employers had 'severed' their feet and kept them at a location different from the rest of their bodies, and these young women's working hours were different from those of the residents of the countries they were sent to.

"Unlike in the Melon Elembele family vocations or professions where your day starts with a walk outside your room for the dew of dawn, followed by invocation time and breakfast, a walk on green lawns barefooted certain days, and every afternoon or evening, a walk in the woods chatting with others, receiving instructions from Mawu Sokpolisa and generating ideas for the family's good and therefore a stake in the family's wealth and, in between working a number of hours, those young women distributed had no time for any other thing.

"When Granddad heard of these modern-day 'faithful workers', as their employers called them, we knew they were bond women but with the tag 'faithful' to distinguish them from those of past centuries who also worked tirelessly only for the employer or owner. Our family aircraft was in one country or the other every week for us to know the depths of what the 'faithful' did or not do.

"In one country, twenty-five of us decided to go for pedicure or, as some women in the group, a pedicure and manicure. Anna, my namesake, was assigned to do my manicure and pedicure. From 6:30am the salon was open, till closing time of 9:30pm, and she was indeed 'faithful' to her work. She had ten minutes for breakfast, so as not to collapse out of hunger and not be useful, for a collapsed worker must be left to die in her country and her world, so without breakfast she would possibly have died many months earlier. She had fifteen minutes for quick lunch, but no time for supper. Possibly she would have supper after they closed, we couldn't tell. We thought other manicurists and pedicurists would attend to some of our number, but this was not to be. They all had their numbers to attend to.

"Two hours before close of the salon, a drunken-looking man came drawling at Anna with a sign that said he owned the salon. And they, eight of them, the employees, live off the tips that kind persons give. She did all of us, going over the closing time by one hour. Granddad gave a tip of twenty per head, and because the employer had left, she smiled with her inner being so that her beauty showed, with Granddad remarking that she looked like the seven-star women of Vicrata, who would not want to be admired for their amazing beauty and adornments commended by men.

"She hugged Granddad and kissed each of us women. It was then that I told Granddad that she had only the looks of the seven-star women, but was not a seven-star woman. Granddad adopted her. And she left with us that night on our aircraft, and so also the seven others. That was redemption in one vocation."

"Were you not afraid that your aircraft could have been blocked from leaving for kidnapping someone's faithful workers?" Melon Jnr asked.

"Such employers seek not to fight with law, for whatever they did was against the law. But with Granddad, their physical attacks would be neutralized by Xebiso, the messenger of Mawu Sokpolisa.

"And these young women, while with the employer, had no other rights and lives. They were prisoners of the employer, from work to their sleeping cubicles and again to work, and any communication with others was only at work. They listened to no songs, saw no films, or anything for the eyes outside working hours.

"And when we got to the mansion, each had an apartment of eight hundred square feet, with kitchen, fridge-freezer, and installed 'Melon viewers' for voice and videos across all nations. And they said in their country of birth language, 'Vivio vivio bans,' which they translated as 'Angels, angels visited.' We left them to rest for two days.

"And after that we taught them the rudiments that would be required. We walked on the green lawns barefooted as required with them, experienced the dew of dawn; went into the woods, chatting and hearing Mawu Sokpolisa give instructions to be turned into ideas. And not left out were the twice-daily invocations. And additionally, taught them also was their attendance at work at the set times. Their smiles didn't cease a moment during the many hours of orientation to the Melon Elembele family values, and later adoption. After it all, we made them send correspondence to their relations in their country of birth from which they were initially uprooted.

"Three months later, we travelled again to redeem millions more. We covered twenty-three other service vocations or professions in many countries of the people of the nations and redeemed young women. And thus was added to the Melon Elembele family, thirty-seven million young women through adoption. And those were the millions we found husbands for when we sought permission from Mawu Sokpolisa to grant them every right or goodness ordained for humans, more so women," Anna said. And added, "You have met my human (woman) needs; I will meet your (human) man's needs."

CHAPTER 43

When Granddad spoke or speaks

Jacksonville, FL, USA. November 22, 2017

"The Melon 'viewers' picked men walking along the four perimeter walls of the market with blood oozing from both palms of their hands. Women who were coming out of the market after buying wares, at the sight, rushed back into the market screaming that anybody who stepped on the blood was also doomed. And on hearing the words of the women, various groups formed around each of them to either listen to what had transpired or what the matter could be and how they could overcome by not stepping in the blood when ready to go home.

"There was, after much chatting and weeping, a word from an elderly woman, whose looks were that of a teenager, that the tears of women can wipe away the blood of any man, since women shed their blood when giving birth to any a son and therefore a man when he grew. Assured thus by this woman with the contrasting features, they decided to wait till the market was closed and then shed a tear on the blood and walk home. Unfortunately, nobody thought of the few men from the sight of the Melon 'viewers' who had also gone to trade their wares. At the close of the market, the women shed a tear on the blood, went over and drove home.

"The men – we saw sixty of them as the Melon 'viewers' now assumed different shapes and positions to furnish us with a fuller picture of them – gathered in one location to decide what to do. But at that instant, two of them remembered that a man had visited the market once and mentioned that men who traded in the market often looked at the breasts of women when they bowed slightly to serve or sell to customers from their sitting position on wooden stools, eighteen inches high. And not only that, but took photos of their breasts and sold the photos to the people of the nations in other countries contrary to the gods' instruction that the women of Loofar's breasts can be seen by Loofar men only. He advised that the men of Loofar reaping profits from the wrong act would be detained one day in the market, and their souls would leave them, and by the morning their bodies would be thrown to the vultures and their bones eaten by dogs.

"The two men asked the others whether they had taken the photos, and they answered in the affirmative. The two said, 'We have also taken the photos. We forgot the man's warnings, but you didn't do any wrong directly. You were ignorant. But the ignorant and the forgetful both pay the same price. Let's hold hands in life and die in death, with hands falling out of other hands, to teach others that you could commit a crime or wrong together but in death you'd be alone.'

"The next morning, the next market day, they were all dead. And women, as if they heard of the man's warning, fed them to the vultures. And at the close of the day, the dogs ate their bones and, with no burial in graves, nobody would ever tell of their existence. 'Because they did wrong in Loofar, they had no memorial, and all of them belonged to the people of the nations, and doing wrong was the norm of the people of the nations . . .' my namesake, Anna, said and paused, so Zetumta said above chatting voices, 'That must be the warnings of Granddad Melon.' 'And how did you know this, Zetumta?' Anna asked. And they all answered, 'You have mentioned it before to us in the woods while we were chatting that Mawu Sokpolisa made Granddad issue warnings, commendations, rebukes and corrections wherever he went, and when not heeded to, then judgments followed, and with that destruction of one type or the other.'

"'Then you know of the king who died? And possibly you have heard of the three presidents of three different countries of the people of the nations who fled their countries because they drank the blood of their own people for power, supposedly, and when warned ate their flesh (bodies) also? And you will not have forgotten, also, that before anybody tried to arrest or did any harm to any Melon Elembele family member, the person died the night before the intention could be carried out, because Granddad had warned every leader of the countries of the people of the nations that Mawu Sokpolisa kills the night before any danger would arise against a Melon Elembele member–?'

"Ziina interrupted Anna by a sound, and held Ella's hand and said, 'It was a pleasure to see life in action. Mawu Sokpolisa protecting against those who even erred against us with words. They had instant and just punishment.' 'Oh, yes, the pyramid sisters, that is Ella, Ziina and Anna, arranged in that order in a straight line were witnesses. You who have not witnessed any will also be witnesses in addition to what you can't see with your eyes. But Mawu Sokpolisa, the Xebiso, is real and true. When you see the lightning flashes and hear the thunders across the skies of the countries of the people of the nations, know that that is Mawu Sokpolisa saying, "I reign because everyone hears my thunders, sees my lightning flashes, feels it, smells it and tastes it!' Anna concluded. While Ella added, 'When and wherever Granddad spoke or speaks, you can also speak, because you are an heir or heiress of good things.'

CHAPTER 44

We mourn that Thursday daytime for twelve hours, and the two hours after

Jacksonville, FL, USA. November 23, 2017

"When thousands upon thousands of men and women began to file into the woods in various countries that Thursday at the dawn hours, the woods looked sombre, as if there would be an incident that could change the nature of Earth. The birds of various sizes and colours didn't chirp. They perched as if nothing mattered again.

"And when each woman or man put a leaf from the jasmine trees dotted across each wooded location, between the lips there arose a hesitancy in those jasmine trees of why each leaf was plucked and put between the lips of men and women and whether that Thursday would be their end, as with no more leaves they could not do a photosynthesis to continue living. Oh! Fortunately, they each had two-thirds of their leaves untouched that fluttered when the winds blew once before 6.00am. At that instant, we gently closed our upper and lower lips on the leaf in each mouth. Time rolled slowly by.

"Woods in which we had chatted anytime we were out in the past, were now with no conversation for twelve hours. But we were not restrained from not walking through the woods, standing or sitting on the ground. Many of us, therefore, did all three intermittently. And time began to move swiftly that way. From one hour, we were in the eleventh hour, when the Melon 'viewers' began showing photos of what was happening in each wooded location or non-wooded. Just before the end of the twelve hours, there came on the Melon viewers' screens the total number who had gathered in the woods in all locations where there were Melon Elembele family members. At 6.00pm, each member swallowed the leaf and gave a shout, 'Mawu Sokpolisa, your new Earth we await!'

"Then we saw the sea waves on the Melon viewers as high as the highest mountain on Earth, moving onto buildings and covering them completely. Then followed heaps of sand, such as had never been seen before, being dumped in the flooded areas, but wetness could still be seen on the images being projected. Spellbound at what was happening, each looked with an expression of fear on her or his face.

"But we had not seen the end of nature causing untold destruction. Grasses and trees sprung out of the wet ground, but in a twinkle of an eye, they turned brown and dry and there were sudden lightning strikes as the grasses and threes burst into flames, and the flames burned and burned and then stopped. And out of the grasses and trees stood different coloured grasses and different coloured trees. The rolling Melon viewers showed different fruits, but they were so distant from us, (from each wooded location), that we desired them only with our eyes, but nobody would be able to pluck any to eat, because of their distant location.

"By the close of the further two-hour mark, the Melon viewers were showing other areas uninhabited, because their inhabitants had been destroyed. Then we heard a voice, like it was coming downwards from above our heads, but it entered the Melon viewers' routers and boomed, 'The new Earth without any people of the nations who lived in the various countries in the world. Go and possess and fill my Earth!"

"It was then that Melon Elembele Jnr appeared and stood closer to me and said, 'Mawu Sokpolisa has ended it so soon.' While Golu Goka put his left arm on my shoulder and right hand on my husband's shoulder and said, 'It has been a long expectation. For many years, I had thought that no new Earth would come, but that we would live on the old Earth as new. But it has come. Xebiso, Mawu Sokpolisa, akpenawo, (Thanks).'

"Hubby, those two hours must always be remembered in our family as the two hours that gave us a new Earth," Anna stated.

"That will be another memorial in our family," Melon Elembele Jnr said.

CHAPTER 45

The Melon VidSounder picks sounds and pictures

Jacksonville, FL, USA. November 24, 2017

Three months after the incidents of those two hours – but with a decision made by the Melon Elembele family that a new calendar system be put into place of eight-hour days and sixteen-hour nights, and the days be counted separately from the nights – the Melon VidSounders at five different locations in the heavens began to send regular feeds of pictures and voices clearly understood and discernible. Anna therefore instructed, as is required of wives or sisters, to give reminders to their husbands, that every husband (brother) and the wives (sisters) must move and take an additional four times of space in addition to their existing space.

But Melon Jnr asked how she came by the figure she had quoted.

Surprised, she asked, "Oh! You didn't listen to the voices from the Melon VidSounders, and see the photos from outer space showing locations on Earth uninhabited? Beautiful and awesome locations with freshness of plants and flowers, but not the sprays of perfume from human-created scents. We must live in nature, for we were made to live within nature."

"Ah! I heard the voices, but the pictures or photos were hazy and I was hoping that with a few more days and nights, the photos would be clearer still, and the move can begin. But women who are in tune with a higher being, the divine, see better and hear better and understand better, as they were and are more endowed; but some don't not know of the two-fold endowment, and my Anna is exceptional . . ."

And while he was still speaking, there were sounds like stones dropping from the skies unto the roofs, and those sounds were also coming as live feeds on the Melon VidSounders, so he therefore stopped to listen to both the sound on the roof and the live feeds. They were similar. And Anna mentioned that she had started recording when the first stone fell on the roof. For thirty minutes, they both, like other Melon Elembele family members, focused on the sounds from the two sources, but somehow managed not to miss pictures of tree houses scattered all over, ice houses, sand houses, cloud houses, rain houses and cave houses or rock houses. And as the pictures or photos ceased, so also the sounds from the two sources.

Anna moved closer to the husband and sat in the 'Love' chair with him, but explained that her intention in sitting by him in the 'Love' chair was not for love or things related to it.

"This is not a time for man and a woman to be ensconced in a web, but a time to listen and understand. I want us to listen to the two sounds as recorded. And because they are from two sources (a woman is two because she is also known as number two), the matter has been settled for us to act in accordance with the sounds from the two sources. Sounds are words from Mawu Sokpolisa. But listen attentively, for you must lead, but if you don't want that honour of leading, Mawu Sokpolisa will allow me to lead because Mawu Sokpolisa is sexless and that is why men and women are married to Mawu Sokpolisa, the Xebiso.

Those sounds were from Xebiso: "Tatami, tata, tata, kpakpaaaa, kpokpopooo, kpum, kpummkpumm, poopooooo, rangooooon, gbooo,"

"Hmm! That was the recording," Anna said.

"There were thirty minutes of loud sounds – loud enough for the people of the nations in the various countries of the world to hear, if they were alive to protest against some of us for disturbing their peace of mind because our god Xebiso spoke," Melon Jnr said.

"Ah. This is not the time to speak about those who are dead. They are no more. What is required is understanding of the sounds. I mentioned that sounds are words. What are the words from the sounds from the two sources?" Anna asked.

"Xebiso is the feminine aspect of Mawu Sokpolisa, a mother. And since mothers have awesome understanding and Anna is a mother of mothers, and no other mother is with me, she will give understanding of the sounds into words. Please, a mother, I have tapped you. Be in our stead, for she that is mystery will understand mysteries," Melon Jnr said.

"A family fails when a woman fails or decides not to play her role. I will play my role. It was the divine, Mawu Sokpolisa, who revealed it to you . . .

"And to the meanings of the sounds: 'Find the size of the new world. Divide it equally among the members of the family, so that each member has each type of the various dwellings in addition to their current dwellings. Each member must render unto each of the ten wives (a sister), an hour a night, and six hours he must sleep. And at sunrise and at sunset, each member, men, women and children, must still carry obligations for such times as in the past, before the new or the transformed Earth. And each wife, a child every year, so that by birthing she is renewed and looks fresher and sweeter than the husband (brother). And in ten years, the numbers of children must be like the numbers of the stars that twinkle at night, but the children must twinkle during the daylight hours with their smiles, for smiles are lights of various colours when seen by others. Listen to further sounds and do as commanded'

"Those were the words from the two sounds," Anna said.

"No journey ends well when a woman is not on the journey playing her role as commanded by the divine, Mawu Sokpolisa. And ten for each on the journey, no failings in the Melon Elembele family," Melon Jnr said as to what they in the Melon Elembele family must do from then onwards.

CHAPTER 46

Xebiso Serrawill Finder

Jacksonville, FL, USA. November 25, 2017

Zetumta arrived in the woods to meet and see millions of smiles on the faces of sisters on the darkest night and darkest glow as glistening white. But the laughter by the millions of brothers shook her legs, and she wobbled, and the pyramid sisters rushed to steady her and pulled a chair for her to sit down. They had gathered in the woods to be told of what the pyramid sisters and Zetumta had come up with, with regards to knowing the will of Mawu Sokpolisa and walking in that will every moment of time.

The pyramid sisters stood up, one after the other, and she also did. Then the Melon VidSounders, all five linked up simultaneously, showed the women standing. They assumed a square position and each started saying the same words simultaneously for five minutes and stopped.

There were smiles again at what all four did and that gave whiteness again in the dark. Then four brothers (husbands) stood up, the husband of each of them, and then nine other women stood up behind each brother (husband), making a total of thirty-six wives (sisters) behind the four brothers. Next, moved Ella to stand in front of her brother (husband), followed by Ziina who also stood in front of her brother (husband), Anna was third and stood in front of her brother (husband), and the fourth, Zetumta, she stood in front of her brother (husband).

With one knee bowed by the four sisters (wives), a square object descended from the sky, and when it was at the height level with Ella, the shortest in height, each of them held one corner in her right hand. At that instant was heard music above their heads reciting the names of Mawu Sokpolisa many times over. When that was finished, Ella, Ziina, Anna and Zetumta simultaneously took out a square object from both ears; then they went on both knees and their foreheads touched the ground four times while reciting the words, 'Mawu Sokpolisa, akpenawo (God Almighty, thank you), Mawu Sokpolisa kafukafu (God Almighty, honour), Mawu Sokpolisa kafukafu kple akpedadanawo (God Almighty, honour and thanksgiving).'

The others behind them didn't do likewise simultaneously, and had to be asked by the pyramid sisters and Zetumta to do as they did. The four in front then moved to their chairs and sat down. Those behind them echoed what the four did.

The pyramid sisters and Zetumta stood up again and simultaneously said they would be called the 'square' sisters from then onwards. And again, simultaneously explained that whatever they did as 'square' sisters was possible because they each had in both their ears the square object and could hear whatever Mawu Sokpolisa said through the square object that descended from the skies, (but not the ten others behind each of them because they didn't have the live feeds that the square sisters had). And finally, they, again simultaneously, gave the name of the square object as 'Xebiso Serrawill Finder'.

And before dispersing to go to their various homes, Melon Jnr announced that the Xebiso Serrawill Finder would be made available to each family member in forty-eight hours from their factories in the five locations where each Melon VidSounders relays live feeds to Earth.

He then strangely asked Zetumta if she had a final word to say as she definitely had a revelation when she walked in late.

Zetumta stood up, smiled, showing all her teeth, and all the sisters also smiled, then she said, 'Sisters' smiles in the darkest night are glistening white,' and brothers all laughed, and she said, 'Brothers' laughters are like storms that would make your legs wobble.'

And, as they left the woods, the brothers tried to smile, but theirs were not like the smile of one sister, more so, of those of millions of sisters.

CHAPTER 47

Mawu Sokpolisa answers their questions

Philadelphia, PA, USA. November 26, 2017

Three weeks into a new regime of using the Xebiso Serrawill Finder to hear directly Mawu Sokpolisa's words, three sisters (wives) but not of the same brother (husband) but of three different brothers (husbands), sent a note to Melon Jnr and Golu Goka asking certain questions that related as far back as thirty years before the Thursday incidents that created a new Earth. The two elderly brothers (husbands of other wives) of other sisters wrote back to them to individually ask Mawu Sokpolisa using the Xebiso Serrawill Finder, as it was also for two-way communication not only from Mawu Sokpolisa to them but from each of them to Mawu Sokpolisa. The two elderly brothers further requested of them to communicate the questions and the answers to all members when they got the answers to the questions from Mawu Sokpolisa.

Ziina was the first to communicate her question and answer, the same day as Golu Goka and Melon Jnr replied to them. She spoke to Mawu Sokpolisa as follows: "Thirty years past, I was one of the people of the nations, living in Zemulu country. At night, one time, I had a dream that an apartment I owned near the coast, alongside those of two thousand other people of the nations covering a six-mile square of land, were all washed away by the raging and ravaging sea waves, and only six of us humans didn't lose our lives in addition to our properties.

"When the sea waves reached me just after the destruction of properties of the community I had mentioned the words 'Mawu

Sokpolisa', not knowing that they are the names of a god, and added the words, 'Sea waves stop,' and the raging waves stopped at my feet, and those of the other five where I stood looking at the destruction that was occurring in our presence.

"And it was not even yet one week after the dream that when I was walking home, I missed my way to the apartment, and was walking in circles, not getting my bearings right. It was in that state that I saw sea waves, more than six hundred feet high, flowing against and covering the apartments, and not a sight of them again. And when the sea waves, now about twenty feet high, would have 'swallowed' me and the five others near me, I shouted, 'Ah! Mawu Sokpolisa, sea waves stop!' And the waves stopped near me and those five humans nearest me. They, not having said anything, were only expectant of certain death.

"'Mawu Sokpolisa, I know you as my family, Mawu Sokpolisa,' I said. 'Why did you destroy all our apartments and many thousands of their human occupants, pets and furniture, but saved the five others and me?' Then Mawu Sokpolisa answered me in these words: 'I don't contend with humans to destroy or kill them or destroy their properties. But in contending and wresting with, and from locational (territorial) gods and goddesses, they fight back by destroying humans and their properties, so that there would be no humans to mention my name and for me to rush and save them. You mentioned my name at the time the waves would have taken away your life, and of the five others near you, and I saved you and those five because the waves stopped. I don't destroy or kill, but as I move further on Earth seeking other locations and people to come under my authority, the existing gods and goddesses destroy and kill, leaving themselves only under my subjection, but not human beings.'

"When Mawu Sokpolisa answered thus, then I understood that humans must not blame Mawu Sokpolisa for deaths and destruction. And dear sisters and brothers, that is the answer from Mawu Sokpolisa to my question.

Awhile later, but before the close of that day, Abish (a sister) communicated her question and answers to all brothers and sisters: "I, Abish, asked Mawu Sokpolisa as to why Mawu Sokpolisa expected a certain moral conduct of the Melon Elembele family but not of all people, including the people of the nations living in the various countries in the world, as that was discriminatory.

"And Mawu Sokpolisa gave the following answer: 'The unknowing have excuses of not knowing. They know another and they don't have excuses with that other. But if they get to know Mawu Sokpolisa, when Mawu Sokpolisa enters among as their Mawu Sokpolisa, then will they no more have excuses for doing the contrary; that of another god or goddess. I, therefore, do not discriminate. I do not judge them with the same standard as those who have heard my words and my name.'

"My dear sisters and brothers, that was Mawu Sokpolisa's answer to my question given out for your education."

The third sister, Guna, communicated her question and answer when the brothers and sisters in most locations would have been fast asleep, saying, "My question to Mawu Sokpolisa was, 'Why, Mawu Sokpolisa have you allowed the wicked to continue in their wickedness and yet there was prosperity for them?' And Mawu Sokpolisa answered: 'When they came to their locations to live, there was a god and goddess dwelling there, and they taught humans, some of the people of nations in the various countries of the world, their ways (gods or goddesses), and they copied them and lived as such. What the Earth promised to give them they will receive, and continue to receive, till I reach out to them with my name and words, and if they continue to act as the god and goddess that had taught them, then will their prosperity cease.'

When the three brothers who had also written to Golu Goka and Melon Jnr woke up the next day, they realized that the three sisters had asked Mawu Sokpolisa questions the same as theirs, and felt constrained not to ask since the answer would be the same, as Mawu Sokpolisa is consistent in words.

And from that day, when Mawu Sokpolisa answered their questions, then those family members who saw Mawu Sokpolisa as high-handed and a murderer, changed their minds to say that Mawu Sokpolisa was benevolent, for the new Earth came about because the gods and goddesses of the people of the nations caused the destruction of their properties and themselves, not that we 'mourned' for Mawu Sokpolisa to kill them.

And none of them even mentioned the name of Mawu Sokpolisa accidentally to save some.

ISBN 978-1-912505-17-3